PUEBLO INTRIGUE

PUEBLO INTRIGUE
A JOURNEY OF FAITH

DON CRAWFORD

TYNDALE HOUSE PUBLISHERS
WHEATON, ILLINOIS

Coverdale House Publishers
London and Eastbourne, England

Distributed in Canada by
Home Evangel Books Ltd.
Toronto, Ontario

DEDICATION

The U.S.S. *Pueblo* (AGER-2)

DUANE HODGES, Damage Controlman 3
in memoriam

Officers

Lloyd Bucher, Commander
Lt. Edward R. Murphy, Jr.
Lt. Stephen Harris
Lt. J.G. Timothy Harris
Lt. J.G. F. Carl Schumacher, Jr.
Chief Warrant Officer Gene Lacy

Men

Rogelio Abelon
Michael Alexander
Rizalino Aluague
Wayne Anderson
Richard Arnold
Charles Ayling
Don Bailey
Herman Baldridge
Richard Bame
Peter Bandera
Michael Barrett
Ronald Berens
Howard Bland
Rushel Blansett
Ralph Bouden
Paul Brusnahan
Willie Bussell
Armando Canales
Robert Chicca
Charles Crandell
Bradley Crowe
Rodney Duke
Steven Ellis
Victor Escamila
Policarpo Garcia

Francis Ginther
Monroe Goldman
John Grant
Gerald Hagenson
Robert Hammond
Lee Roy Hayes
John Higgins
Robert Hill
Sidney Karnes
James Kell
Earl Kisler
Norbert Klepac
Anthony Lamantia
Peter Langenberg
Charles Law, Jr.
James Layton
Wendell Leach
Harry Lewis
David McClarren
Ralph McClintock
Lawrence Mack
Roy Maggard
Larry Joe Marshall
William Massie

John Mitchell
Clifford Nolte
Michael O'Bannon
Donald Peppard
Alvin Plucker
Ralph Reed
Dale Rigby
David Ritter
Steven Robin
Richard Rogala
Ramon Rosales
E. Stuart Russell
William Scarborough
James Shepard
John Shilling
John Shingleton
Norman Spear
Charles Sterling
Angelo Strano
Lawrence Strickland
Kenneth Wadley
Steven Woelk
Elton Wood
Darrell Wright

Civilians

Harry Iredale III

Dunnie Tuck

CONTENTS

ACKNOWLEDGEMENTS

Although it bears one byline, this book could not be the result of a single effort. The author recognizes and is indebted to the great number of persons required to produce a work of this nature. They all deserve, and have, his sincere appreciation even though they cannot be mentioned individually. Special note must be made, however, of the following:

KENNETH N. TAYLOR, publisher of Tyndale House, for his help and understanding throughout the necessarily accelerated procedure.

MRS. DENISE WOLFF, who first expressed the need for such a book and whose contributions were considerable—researching, interviewing, encouraging.

ROBERT L. OWEN, California free-lance writer and friend of the author, who initiated contact with the *Pueblo* crewmen, opening the way for subsequent interviews.

LIEUTENANT STEPHEN HARRIS and COMMUNICATIONS TECHNICIAN FIRST-CLASS FRANCIS GINTHER, who, along with their wives, opened their hearts and minds to the author in order that the *Pueblo* story could be told.

MRS. ELEANOR HARRIS, Lieutenant Harris's mother, whose careful recording of information about the capture and captivity of the *Pueblo* and of her own personal involvement proved exceptionally beneficial.

JOHN M. ROBINSON, whose skillful and complete handling of editorial responsibilities of the *Christian Times* relieved the editor for his role as author.

MRS. ALICE LUBBERS, invaluable research assistant, who typed and retyped the manuscript with a composure as cool as the typing was clean.

MRS. DONNA BIRKEY, whose efficiency in transcribing the formidable amount of recorded conversations into typewritten documents expedited the preparation of the manuscript.

ROBERT HAWKINS and EDYTHE DRAPER, who engineered the speedy but efficient operation demanded in the production of a book with a relevant message.

MRS. CLARETA CRAWFORD, who kept five live-wire children out of the author's hair and who, although she receives last position in this list of benefactors, retains first place in the author's affections.

AUTHOR'S NOTE

"There was a revivalist impulse to religion." With these words *Newsweek* magazine, in its February 24, 1969, issue, described one aspect of the confinement in North Korea of the crew of the U.S.S. *Pueblo*. The assessment was based on testimony given by the crewmen before a Navy court of inquiry, as well as on the magazine's own research. Independent investigation preceding the writing of this book suggested that most of the crew were actually sustained by much more than an impulsive reliance on God. It was in fact the certain revelation that God was able to overcome all the forces of evil confronting the *Pueblo* crewmen that prompted the account given here.

It must be stressed that this work is by no means an attempt to tell the full story of the *Pueblo*. It is, more explicitly, the adventure in faith that was lived by two of the eighty-two survivors of Communistic duplicity and terror. The two—an officer and an enlisted man—are representative of the crewmen interviewed, all of whom expressed a common appraisal: without God the ordeal would have been impossible.

In compiling data for the book, the author discovered that human memory is a volatile commodity. Discrepancies often turned up in the various reports about specific occurrences as they were remembered in interviews or presented in public testimony. The author was forced in some cases to rely on a judgmental reconstruction based on his own intensive investigation and his personal experience as a crewman aboard a U.S. naval vessel (which, incidentally, operated in the waters surrounding the Korean peninsula during the United Nations police action of the 1950's). It is possible, of course, that an episode recorded here would receive a different interpretation from another observer.

Extensive efforts were made, nonetheless, to contact every person involved in the action that makes up the following account, to insure that what has been presented here is basically accurate and true to the nature of the incident. If the story that follows contains error, may the very human author be forgiven. If the book succeeds in making real the faithfulness of a loving Creator, may God alone gain the glory.

DON CRAWFORD,
Carol Stream, Illinois

If your faith remains strong after being tried in the test tube of fiery trials, it will bring you much praise and glory and honor on the day of Christ's return.

1 Peter 1:7,
Living New Testament

1

JANUARY 23

The waters of the Sea of Japan were cold, gray, and still. The eighty-three men aboard the AGER-2 welcomed the calm. It gave them a rest from the washtub stability their ungainly craft normally provided. In spite of the unusually smooth waters, however, lookouts at their posts around the small vessel were particularly watchful.

The ship was near unfriendly shores that January morning and—despite its pretentious designation, "Auxiliary, General, Environmental Research"—she was not gifted with a great deal of speed. Just the day before two North Korean boats, apparently fishing vessels, had circled her. The captain had broken radio silence to send a situation report to headquarters in Japan. For some reason Japan could not be raised until fourteen hours later; otherwise, everything seemed to be going well.

But now the ship was stopped dead to test the temperature and salinity of the water, important factors for accurate sonar findings, and the slow pitching of the ship a few miles off of North Korea increased the feeling of uneasiness.

Back in Bremerton, Washington, while the vessel was being outfitted, relatives of the crew had been told that the old Army freighter was being equipped for oceanographic studies. But the crew knew better. True, two civilian oceanographers were aboard, but the detachment of twenty-eight communications technicians who manned the complex electronic equipment weren't there just

1

to check the geography of the ocean bottom. The CTs worked in a triple-locked compartment; the hardware they used could do a lot more than sample sea water, if the scuttlebutt was reliable.

The rumors were that the twin antennas mounted forward of the wheelhouse could locate and identify distant radar and radio sources; that the domelike direction finders and sensors on the foremast, used to eavesdrop on radio communications, were so sensitive they could read signals bouncing from the troposphere; that far-sighted cameras could see a ship's single-wire antenna at 5,000 yards; that hidden beneath the waterline were other supersecret pieces of equipment—sonar domes, hydrophones, subsurface antennas—that could gather and analyze electronic signals for miles around.

But whatever the equipment was designed for, it seemed to give sufficient reason to stay clear of the territorial waters of the Democratic People's Republic of Korea, which was somewhere in the hazy horizon off the starboard side. The chart in the quartermaster's shack put them seventeen miles off the nearest land, a five-mile safety margin against North Korea's self-imposed twelve-mile territorial limit.

Probably far enough. It was the maiden voyage of the U.S.S. *Pueblo* since its conversion to a surveillance ship, however, and no one really knew how far "far enough" was. The ship had left Sasebo, Japan, only twelve days before, hardly long enough to test all of its sophisticated gear.

Despite the mass of intelligence equipment aboard, some things still had to be done "old Navy." The log—headed in typical square letters "23 JAN 68"—required notations by human hand, just as in the days of John Paul Jones. Lookouts provided human eyesight to define whatever the always-probing radar might discover. But neither lookout nor radar had caught anything that morning.

It was noon when Seaman Ramon Rosales reported to the

bridge to relieve the port lookout. "Anything happening?" he asked.

"I think radar's got something, but it's probably just another fishing boat," he was told. A slight shiver traveled Rosales' lean shoulders. Considering the position of the *Pueblo* and the eerie calm that accompanies a stopped ship, he couldn't help wondering . . .

His thoughts were interrupted as the radar shack asked for visual confirmation of an approaching surface vessel. Quartermaster Chuck Law called the wardroom and told Commander Lloyd Bucher about the ship . . . "seven or eight miles away, closing fast."

"Take a fresh check on our position," Bucher replied. While this was being done, the captain trotted to the flying bridge. He took the ship's "big eyes"—the 22-inch binoculars—and scanned the horizon. There it was. A Soviet SO-1 flying the North Korean naval ensign.

Bucher was not overly disturbed. Harassment was an expected hazard of sailing these waters. He had anticipated it since he began this tour—scheduled for one month—off North Korean waters. A few minutes later as the subchaser approached, Pete Bucher could see that its crew was at general quarters. Sailors on deck manned 57-millimeter cannon, submachine guns, and carbines. The Korean vessel completely circled the *Pueblo*. It circled again, closer this time. Finally it came alongside and hoisted international signal flags. "What is your nationality?" the message read.

"Hoist the ensign," Bucher commanded.

At the sight of the American flag being raised, the Koreans on the bridge of the subchaser began to jump around excitedly. The action was so animated it would have been humorous to the Americans had they been observing it under other circumstances.

"Light off the main engines," Bucher ordered calmly. "Prepare to answer all bells." The orders were relayed to the engine room.

Bucher reminded himself of the orders he had received ashore: to ignore harassment and to avoid any overt action against the North Koreans or Russians. He wondered momentarily if he should call general quarters, but decided against it. Having the men at their battle stations could be interpreted in the wrong way by the Koreans. Anyway, the *Pueblo's* weaponry was too meager, even for a bluff. It consisted of two .50-caliber machine guns, a few anti-swimmer concussion grenades, ten submachine guns, and one carbine. And the crew, limited for the task the ship had been assigned, had not been fully trained in using the armament. As if to settle the matter, a look at the two machine guns revealed they were encased not only in their canvas covers but also by heavy coatings of ice.

Another signal from the subchaser: "Heave to or I will fire."

"Tell them we're in international waters," Bucher ordered. The signals went up.

As the realization came upon the captain that the Koreans might be meaning to do more than simply harass the *Pueblo*, he pondered the destruction of the valuable intelligence gear. He turned to Chief Warrant Officer Gene Lacy, his engineer. "Any possibility that we could scuttle?"

"Not very quickly. Anyway, we're standing in only thirty fathoms. They could easily use divers to retrieve our equipment."

When Bucher learned the temperature of the water was only a little above freezing, he abandoned the plan. His crew wouldn't have a chance in the bitter cold.

He didn't have time to consider his next move. Action by the Koreans dictated an almost automatic series of survival tactics. The subchaser was joined by four Russian-built P-4 torpedo boats, one of which was approaching the *Pueblo*. On its deck a group of men stood armed and in readiness. A boarding party.

Bucher ordered the *Pueblo* underway and started toward the open sea. He smiled grimly at the thought of a chase. At its full speed of twelve knots, the *Pueblo* was a helpless tortoise surrounded by fast-paced sharks. Hoping to buy a little time from the inquisitive Koreans, he had signals hoisted that read, "Thank you for your consideration. I am departing the area."

As the American prize moved away, two Korean P-4s began crisscrossing in front of the *Pueblo's* bow. A second subchaser joined the harassers, took a position off the *Pueblo's* tail, and signaled: "Heave to or I will fire." Bucher ignored the signal, ordering the engine room to maintain full speed.

Seconds later every man aboard the *Pueblo* became fully conscious of the North Koreans' intentions. A burst of fire from the subchaser's cannon tore into the American vessel, damaging the navigational mast and spraying the flying bridge with shrapnel.

"They got the captain!" someone shouted.

But Commander Bucher picked himself up. "I'm okay," he said, ignoring the pain in his punctured legs and hips. Three others, also wounded, were getting up as a lookout yelled, "Aircraft! Ten o'clock! Astern!" Two MIG jets screamed in, unloading a salvo of rockets.

A collective sigh of relief rose from the bridge as the rockets plunged harmlessly into the water ahead of the *Pueblo*. But more cannon fire from the subchasers and machinegun fire from the P-4s began to rain on the American ship. In a quick telephone conversation with Intelligence Officer Lieutenant Steve Harris in the communications shack, Bucher learned that radioteletype circuit with Japan was open and that the destruction of classified material had begun.

"Better destroy the equipment, too," Bucher yelled.

Harris had no time then to think about the frequent conversations he had had with Bucher about security: Who was responsible for the intelligence equipment? Did the captain's authority overlap his responsibility for the classified material? What would actually constitute a threat of compromise? How would destruction be done? He knew Commander Bucher had tried repeatedly to obtain a destruct system before the trip began, but his request had been turned down. The mission wasn't that dangerous, he'd been told. An image of the letters both he and Bucher had prepared seeking clarification flashed quickly through his mind. They were in a pouch in the captain's safe.

Getting rid of the classified material was a big order. There must have been a ton of bound documents and written directives. The two shredders used for routine disposal of superseded directives were hopeless. One wouldn't work and the other was too slow. Feverishly, the men set to ripping the documents apart and tearing the pages into bits by hand.

What to do with the scraps? Mattress covers were grabbed off bunks in a nearby sleeping compartment and the paper was stuffed into them.

"If you guys know any prayers," CT First-Class Frank Ginther called without mockery, "now is the time to say them." No one laughed.

On the bridge at that moment Captain Bucher faced the grim prospect of losing his ship and crew. He was looking into the uncovered torpedo tubes of the P-4 alongside.

"All stop," he ordered. As the ship slowed, the enemy fire died down.

In the lull Bucher checked on the destruction of the secret material and electronic gear—which was proceeding apace—and heard that the Navy base in Yokosuka was receiving continuing reports on their situation.

The subchaser was signalling again: "Follow me. I have a pilot on board." A look at the menacing enemy ships surrounding him confirmed the sincerity of the demand. "Ahead one-third," he ordered the engine room and told helmsman Ron Berens to bring the ship around.

The slow pace of their captive vessel didn't suit the North Koreans. The P-4 came alongside and an officer on its deck motioned to the *Pueblo's* bridge. It was obvious he wanted the

Americans to increase speed. Bucher's answer was a shrug of the shoulders and a gesture of incomprehension.

A call for the captain. On the telephone Harris told him, "We're not going to be able to destroy all this paper! I think we'd better let Yokosuka know." Bucher agreed. "All stop," he commanded.

Below decks axes and sledge hammers were flying into the expensive electronic gear. The hand-shredding operation had created a sea of debris underfoot. Mattress covers and their contents were being weighted for dumping. An attempt to set the papers afire had created smoke-laced confusion. Fireman Duane Hodges grabbed the small equipment kept in a safe outside the captain's cabin and started for the deck. Outside it was apparent the Koreans were becoming impatient.

"They're going to open fire—" The warning was lost in ear-shattering blasts from the subchaser.

"They got Hodges!"

"Call a corpsman!"

"My God! Right in the gut!"

Under a rake of machinegun fire Commander Bucher ordered the *Pueblo's* engines ahead one-third. Their only hope now was to get some outside help. During the next several minutes, punctuated with reports on Hodges' condition and the activity aboard the surrounding vessels, Bucher was engaged in a desperate conversation with headquarters via teletype in the communications compartment. "How about a little help out here? These guys mean business."

In came the reply: "Word has gone to all authorities. The Commander of Naval Forces in Japan is requesting assistance. What key list do you have left?"

Bucher was sure most of the key list, the classified cryptographic material, was destroyed. What concerned him then was a report from a lookout: "P-4 approaching starboard with fenders rigged!" He looked at the oncoming boat, rubber tubes and rope mats draping its port bow, an armed boarding party on its deck. "Are you sending assistance?" he asked headquarters.

"Please advise if your communications spaces will be entered," was the reply.

The P-4 edged toward the *Pueblo's* bow. Bucher continued to make his report. "Have been requested to follow into Wonsan. Have three wounded and one man with leg blown off. Have not used any weapons nor uncovered .50-caliber machine gun. Destroying all key lists and as much electronic equipment as possible . . . Have sustained small wound in rectum . . . Do not intend to offer any resistance." Such action then would not only have been against his orders, it would have been futile. He returned to his report: "Will keep this up until the last minute. Sure could use some help now . . . Over to you."

Yokosuka's answer this time seemed less complacent. "Roger, roger. Doing all we can. Everyone really turning to and figure by now Air Force got some birds winging your way."

That was good news. But they'd have to hurry. Calmly Bucher made his reply. "Sure hope so. We're pretty busy with this destruction . . . can't see for the smoke." He instructed CT First-Class Don Bailey to continue the teletype report until it became necessary to destroy the equipment. The Koreans were signalling again. They wanted him to bring his ship to a stop.

The P-4 bumped against the *Pueblo.* A rope was tossed over her lifeline and secured. With the jets overhead, the two sub-chasers, and the three torpedo boats surrounding their captive, Koreans armed with submachine guns scrambled aboard.

Word was quickly passed to stop the destruct operation. It was too late now. With futile shrugs, the American sailors obeyed the Korean instructions to gather on the well deck. Hospital Corps-man Herman Baldridge and Commissaryman Ralph Reed were giving as much comfort as they could to Duane Hodges. A Korean tried to order them away. It was hopeless trying to communicate with him. Surely he could see how badly wounded Hodges was. They turned back to their work.

In the wheelhouse Bucher was confronted by armed guards and a Korean officer who spoke English. Orders were given to the helmsman and the engine room. The *Pueblo* proceeded toward Wonsan.

A few minutes earlier, at 2:32 P.M., Naval headquarters in Japan had received a final teletype message from the *Pueblo*. Normally a routine transmission, this time it had a hollow tone: "Going off the air." The spirit of the vessel and the life of Duane Hodges had escaped before the *Pueblo* reached the enemy port.

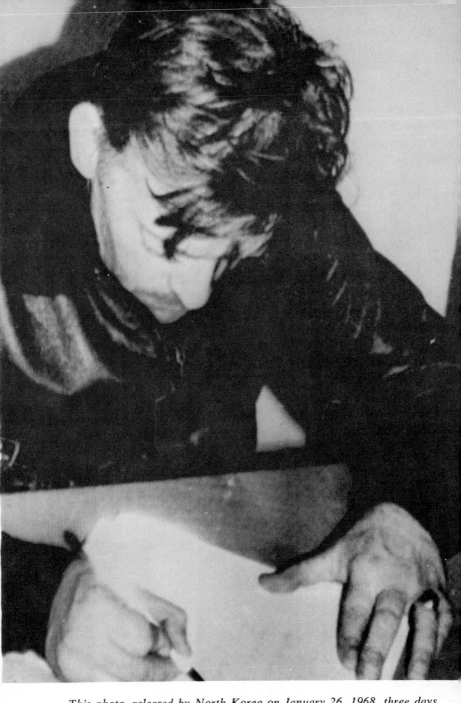

This photo, released by North Korea on January 26, 1968, three days after the Pueblo capture, purportedly shows Commander Bucher writing a confession. Signs of an extreme ordeal are evident in his appearance.

2

ALONE

He raised his hand to knock on the door, then drew it back. Except for the circumstances it would have seemed ridiculous: knocking on the *inside* of a door for permission to come *out*. But Lieutenant Harris checked his laughter. He had experienced enough "punishment for naughty deeds" to know better than to tempt the hallway guard, who was particularly sensitive about being made fun of. Anyway, he had virtually exhausted his excuses for leaving the room. One could make only so many trips to the bathroom without arousing suspicion. And then the guard might not let you in if someone was already there, even though the combination bathroom, washroom, and laundry room served forty men. With the drains of all three sinks usually clogged and the other facility designed for Orientals more adept at squatting, it really wasn't too inviting anyway. So Harris stayed in his room, which wasn't much to inspire meditation, either. Four bare plaster walls with a door on one side, a window on the other, and a bare lightbulb in the ceiling. A bed, a nightstand, a chair. He had already paced off the room too many times. It always came out twelve by eighteen feet. The cracks in the wood floor never lost their mocking, toothless grin. The stack of literature on the table didn't excite him, even though the Korean handling of the English language was often amusing. But it only told him of American atrocities or imperialist capitalistic aggression, and he was tired of reading the same theme.

11

The window held promise, however. Through it he could see the distant mountains, covered with snow when they arrived, now green; and the closer village with its strident loudspeakers blasting anti-American "information" at the ignorant citizens; and, closer still, the rice paddies. Through the window he had seen the farmers plant their rice, saw it grow, and now could witness the harvest.

His food (the foul-smelling fish dubbed *filet of sewer trout,* the weak soup called *creme de garbage* by the crew) was brought to his room. So he spent much of his time alone, as did the other *Pueblo* officers. All had perfected the fine art of daydreaming. During one chance meeting, Engineer Gene Lacy told Harris, "I finished rebuilding my '36 Ford this morning. I think I'll sand it down and paint it this afternoon." Lt.J.G. Skip Schumacher told him at an evening meeting, which the Koreans permitted, that in a six-weeks mental marathon he had designed a $56,000 dream house "until the skipper ruined it by telling me what the taxes would be."

For Steve Harris the mental diversion centered around reliving past experiences. He was able to recall almost every portion of his life from childhood on. Most of his memories—except of his father's death nine years before, and those accumulated the past eight months—were pleasant.

Having discarded his broad New England dialect, he referred to himself as an "improper Bostonian," but his credentials remained impeccable. The Family Harris had come to Jamestown in 1614. Three of his forefathers had fought in the Revolutionary War; his mother was a descendant of *Mayflower* Pilgrim John Alden. Stephen Robert Harris was born and reared in suburban Boston. He was a Harvard graduate, with a speaking facility in several foreign languages. He dabbled in the esoteric history of streetcars and loved Rachmaninoff. Several of his forebears had been sailing captains. His mother's family motto, *Amor Patriae Exitat,* inspired him, for love of his country did indeed excite him. At Harvard he participated in the Naval Reserve Officer Training

Corps, and when he graduated in 1960 he accepted his commission and looked forward to a naval career.

Harris had time now to relive his early Navy days, first as a line officer aboard the U.S.S. *Grand Canyon,* a destroyer tender, and later aboard the destroyer *Forrest Sherman.* On these ships he had made his first two cruises, both to the Mediterranean. He recalled with satisfaction his rise in rank from Ensign to Lieutenant Junior Grade to Lieutenant; he hoped soon to be Lieutenant Commander—if he got out of this.

In 1963 things changed for the better in many ways for the tall, dark-haired officer. That was the year he was transferred to Navy Language School in Washington, D. C., where he learned Russian, was cleared for naval intelligence, and later met the beautiful secretary who became his wife. A single incident, however, stood out in Harris's mind as the turning point of his life.

He had gotten acquainted with Lt. Stan Beach, a chaplain for the destroyer squadron to which he was attached. Beach invited Harris to his home in Newport one evening for a meal and a chat about Harris's duties as the destroyer's Protestant lay leader. Harris recalled that he hadn't been enthusiastic about being hymnbook custodian. The prospect of a sermon from Chaplain Beach didn't excite him either. But he went.

Sure enough, after the meal Beach brought up the subject of religion. Harris was intrigued by what Stan had to say, however. It was the first time that he had been confronted with the idea of Christ dying for his shortcomings. He had been brought up in churches, but he had never had the meaning of salvation explained to him the way Beach did: that God, not man, created a new person out of the sincere believer who put his trust in Jesus Christ. It sounded so simple; yet the prospect of his becoming "changed" was so formidable, Harris was afraid to make the decision. He left the house in a state of inward turmoil.

In Naples Harris had met a man known for his unsavory reputation who had suddenly made a remarkable moral rehabilitation.

His explanation had been, "I accepted Christ as my Savior." This had impressed the young naval officer, although he didn't fully understand it. Harris had always kept his own outward appearance above reproach. There could be no dramatic change even if he did make a commitment to Christ.

But he had the gnawing feeling that something inside him *was* changing. It was unnerving. The faith that Stan Beach had explained was too uncomplicated to be a deep religion, but too comforting in its assurance of forgiveness of sins (even the hidden ones) to be ignored. Harris couldn't get the thing out of his mind. Were his efforts to tailor his own life—though his record was enviable—worthless? Could it really be that God loved him enough to conquer the temptations and discouragements of life through his Son? And was it really true that Steve Harris could have this —and everlasting life—merely by saying "yes" to Jesus Christ? The Bible verses Stan had referred him to certainly seemed to indicate it was all true. When he could stand it no longer, he had gone unannounced to the Beach home.

Mrs. Beach answered his knock. "We're being transferred," she said, explaining the boxes and crates that greeted him. She called her husband, who was in the attic packing.

"Am I glad I caught you!" Steve began as Beach entered the living room.

"What's up?"

"Tell me again about becoming a Christian."

The two were soon praying together amid the trunks and packing boxes. According to his Navy records, Steve Harris was born on March 31, 1938, in Melrose, Massachusetts. His memory recorded a second birth: October 3, 1963, in Newport, Rhode Island.

It was as a new Christian, Harris remembered, staring languidly now at the Korean farmers in their rice paddies, that he became involved in the Officers' Christian Union and with the Navigators. Both groups had helped him in Scriptural research which increased his understanding of the faith. He was grateful now for the Bible passages he had memorized, and for the friendships he had made.

At an OCU Bible study meeting, he had met Gus Uotinen, a dentist and major in the Army Medical Corps. Eight months later he found out about Gus's sister. He was leaving a Sunday evening service at the Fourth Presbyterian Church in Bethesda, Maryland, when he met Gus in the narthex. With him was a doe-eyed butternut blonde who, Steve knew, was not his wife. Harris felt the same fever creep into his face now as he recalled the meeting. There were the introductions. "My sister, Esther . . . Steve Harris."

Steve learned that Esther was one of three children of a Finnish Lutheran minister; that she was a secretary for a trade association in Washington; that she enjoyed the dynamic evangelical messages of Fourth Presbyterian's pastor, Richard Halverson, although she was not a member as was Steve; that she preferred her coffee black, liked semi-classical music; and, no, she wasn't engaged or anything like that.

Harris recalled the courtship . . . their marriage in December of 1966, performed by Esther's father . . . and the five months they had enjoyed together before the *Pueblo* sailed—marred only by their first brief separation. Steve had gone to Bremerton in March to command the intelligence detachment aboard the surveillance ship. Esther had stayed behind in Washington. They tried to tell themselves it would be temporary, that it was the life of anyone in the Navy to be away for long periods of time. But two weeks was all either could stand. Esther joined Steve in Bremerton, where they had found fulfillment in finding a house, buying things for their home that they "could always have," and sharing evenings together. He could not know then how precious those simple experiences were to become to him. Soon it was time to sail to San Diego for training and, in the fall of 1967, on to the Sea of Japan.

As his mental journey continued, Harris lived again the agonizing trip across the Pacific with the 176-foot *Pueblo* at the mercy of the ocean waves. Determined to share his faith with others, the

Intelligence Officer, again an unofficial chaplain for the crew, arranged a worship service for the first Sunday out. He recalled now his disappointment at the turnout. Only two showed up. Of course, there were good reasons. The crew was small and many were on duty. Not a few—even some of the old salts— were seasick from the constant undulation of the vessel. But those who could have come didn't. Harris decided there just wasn't enough interest and abandoned any further attempt to have a service. He wondered now, separated as he was from the crew except for brief conversations during an exercise period, if he should have persisted. But he knew he could not deliver what was not willingly received.

Why, he wondered, turning from the window and fingering the Communist magazines on the table, was it easier to think about the distant past than to recall what had happened in the last half year? Yet think about it he must—relive it, dissect it, piece it together—if he was ever to solve the riddle of why he was here and what God wanted him to do about it. He made his mind return to the twenty-third of January. His view of the *Pueblo's* capture was limited since he had spent most of the two and a half hours in the confines of the communications compartment. There was the blast of enemy fire . . . the destruction of the valuable equipment . . . the slow process of shredding the secret documents . . . the chaotic attempt to burn them . . . the aborted dumping . . . Hodges' death . . . the boarding. It had all happened too fast. The mental images were many and they crowded upon each other, making it hard to settle on the correct sequence.

As the *Pueblo* had made its somber journey to Wonsan harbor, Harris grabbed a Bible from his desk and stuffed it inside his jacket. If the Air Force didn't come to their rescue soon his Bible could prove very helpful. Most of the crew had gotten the word from whispered conversation that the Air Force was sending help. But . . . when?

As darkness fell over the Sea of Japan, hope died. There was to follow a long period of silence concerning any American action, Harris now well knew, and fear that the *Pueblo* had been forgotten was a monster that had to be battled daily.

Since the captives had been blindfolded, it was difficult to tell the time of day that they were led, stumbling, off the docked vessel. Harris knew that it had taken several hours to reach port. The docking maneuver must have been handled poorly, judging from the impact. While yet on board Harris had been given a preview of the treatment the crew might expect from Korean hands. They were being moved from the well deck to a sleeping compartment when his Bible was discovered. A guard pointed his submachine gun at Harris's middle and shouted in Korean. Harris drew in his breath. The guard jabbed his hand at the lieutenant's jacket, pulled it up brusquely, and grabbed the Bible. It was the last Harris saw of it. Soon enough he would discover the guard's action was a display of mild annoyance.

Before they made their final departure from the *Pueblo,* the Americans were searched and their hands trussed tightly against their chests. They could hear, but not see, the hissing, jeering, spitting crowd of Korean citizens awaiting their arrival. Still blindfolded and bound, they were loaded onto buses. After a short drive the Americans, silent in fear and wonder, were unloaded and placed aboard a train for an all-night ride—the blindfolds still in place, their hands still tied. They arrived in Pyongyang, the Democratic People's capital city, before dawn. When the train came to its final stop, guards removed the blindfolds and untied their prisoners. Harris remembered the ache in his eyes from the brightness of the flashbulbs and the television lights as they were marched from the station.

Not far from the scene of the propaganda picture-taking was a barracks, their home for a month. Except for Commander Bucher—no one knew what might be happening to him—the men were assigned to their quarters, four to a room. Each man had a wooden-slat bed with a loose cotton mattress on which were placed a rice-shell pillow, muslin sheets, and a thin woolen blanket. Each was also furnished with a wooden chair, crudely made as all the equipment they were to encounter seemed to be. A bare lightbulb hung from the ceiling. It burned night and day. The window was covered; what was on the other side they would not know, but they would hear the passing of trains, the marching of troops, and the playing of children.

Harris estimated his room to be about fourteen by sixteen feet. With him were Gunner's Mate Ken Wadley, Corpsman Herman Baldridge, and Fireman Tom Massie. As they were herded into their rooms, they were told in English to go to sleep.

Sleep did not come easily despite the restless nighttime train ride. Later in the morning—Harris guessed around eleven o'clock —he and the other officers were called together. They faced a Korean general and several other Korean officers.

"You are guilty of trespassing the territorial waters of the Democratic People's Republic of North Korea," they were told through an interpreter.

All six officers denied the charge.

The general glowered. He spoke a sentence in Korean. Before the interpretation came the Americans knew they would be harsh words.

"You will all be *executed,*" he spit out the word. "Today at sundown."

That was all. Harris felt again the numbness that swept over him at that moment.

Baldridge, Massie, and Wadley looked up as Harris re-entered. "They're going to shoot us today," he told them. He realized the severity of the sentence then as he saw the reaction among the men. Sweat appeared on their faces. His own throat was dry.

"Well, they sure brought us a long way to do it," one of the men broke the silence.

Then it dawned on Harris that he would soon be with the

Christ he had come to know less than five years before. Now, in his solitary room with the appointed execution long since passed, Harris could still recall his elation at the thought. He had wondered briefly about the painful way their deaths might be accomplished, but the realization that he would soon be in heaven had buoyed him through the day. He remembered thinking about leaving a bride and a widowed mother, and praying for them. "You're able to take care of them, I know, Lord," he had said silently, "but I do hate the thought of leaving them. Please comfort them." For a moment he wondered if he should feel so happy about being in the presence of God when it would surely cause grief for the ones he would leave behind.

Conversation in the room had been limited. Each man seemed intent on pursuing his own thoughts. But in the afternoon, when Harris noticed one of the men fidgeting uneasily, he knew he had to share his Savior with them. He prayed for the right words, for he would never have another chance to give them this information.

"You know," he began, "for a Christian this can be the greatest moment." The trio looked at him. "Not long ago I learned what Christ had done for me, personally, when he died on the cross. All I had to do to receive forgiveness for every wrong I had done —and at the same time receive eternal life—was to accept him. Regardless of what you may have done in your lives, you don't have to worry about a thing when you face death if you accept Jesus Christ as your Lord and Savior." The men looked at him in silence. "Just pray to God in his name and believe in him, and you'll live with him forever."

Harris couldn't tell what was going on in their minds. No one said a word. It wasn't until later that he was to hear Baldridge say, "Before the captivity I wasn't what you would call a religious man, but when things really got rough, I turned to prayer. My wife is Japanese. She's not a Buddhist. She believes in God, but I never made much of an effort to help her understand Christianity.

Things are going to be different when we get together again. I want to do all I can to encourage my wife to understand the Christian faith and to embrace it for herself."

As the day took its course and the sun reached toward the horizon, Harris realized as never before that his life was not in his own hands. He had known this before, of course, but now it had been made meaningful to him. At length the sun set. No one had come in to lead them away. Perhaps, he thought, they meant sun *rise* and the interpreter had said the wrong word. He didn't share this possibility with the others; they were in enough fear as it was.

He slept well that night but awakened before sunrise. The midwinter sun took its time coming up. When it finally rose, nothing happened. The whole day, he now recalled, passed just like that. Nothing happened. In the evening they were issued uniforms and toilet articles, and then Harris knew it had been a bluff. The name of the game was Fear.

There was an element of traveling from the sublime to the ridiculous with the issuance of the clothing. The *Pueblo* crew's own uniforms were taken away ("probably to be shot full of holes and displayed every May Day," someone suggested), but they were allowed to keep their watches, jewelry, and grooming utensils. They were given muslin underwear, pajama-like outfits to cover these, sweat suits to go over the pajamas, bulky dark-blue outer garments of thick cotton, and heavy coats. To complete the uniform, they were each given one pair of socks and a pair of canvas shoes.

Thinking about the four weeks they had spent in the Barn, as the crew had christened the building, was not a pleasurable pastime. Harris sat down on his chair, looked briefly at a magazine, then tossed it back on the table. He remembered there was never enough heat in the Barn. The cold cement walls and the drafty, widely cracked floors seemed to defy the meager attempt made by a small radiator to warm the room. The guards were over-eager to find any excuse—a wrinkled bed, a smile of supposed derision, a misunderstood phrase—to "punish" the arrogant Americans. The Korean officers, too, made up reasons to awaken the captives at any hour of the night for questioning or punishment.

The zealous guards were adept at rapid hand blows and boot kicks to almost any part of their adversary's body. The submachine guns slung over their shoulders were frequently brought into the game, either as a threat of immediate execution or as a pummeling stick. Every infliction seemed pre-selected for its painful aftermath or visible bruises, with the goal being a reaction of fear within the Americans.

On the third morning the officers were moved into separate quarters. Only then had it occurred to Harris that the isolation of the officers meant that personnel folders had been studied. The thought of what action might be taken against the intelligence crew disturbed him. His men had been told to cover their mission to friends and relatives, but they had not been told what to do if captured, nor even warned to expect it. None had been trained to face torture. The Navy had considered the surveillance mission off North Korea dangerous only to the point of possible harassment. But at that moment, separated from the men, Harris realized the potential danger, especially to the intelligence crew. And he was the *Pueblo's* chief spy.

His apprehensions were soon translated into actual experience. Within a three-week period the officers and many of the men would be interrogated—probed, prodded, ridiculed, and punished, their lives threatened and their bodies brutalized—until, seeing the futility of denying the Koreans their single consuming pleasure, they would all at length sign confessions so improbable they would prove nothing, except the culpability of their captors.

Harris got up and walked to the window, forcing the unwelcome recollection away.

The move out of the Barn, with its traumatic memories, had been a godsend. Preparations for the transfer to their present

Lieutenant Edward Murphy, Pueblo executive officer, speaks at a press conference held in North Korea. To his left are Commander Bucher and Lieutenant Harris.

Pix

location were made mysteriously, as all Korean action seemed to be undertaken. One day the Americans were simply loaded onto buses and then told they were being moved to another building. Adding to the mystery, all of the windows on the buses were covered except for the drivers' peepholes.

The trip was a short one—perhaps six miles—to the outskirts of Pyongyang. The whitewashed cement building the crewmen entered was a definite improvement over the Barn. The Americans learned later that the structure had been recently erected for the housing of participants in Communist-bloc military contests. Ranges and targets for rifle shooting, hand-grenade throwing, and pistol matches were nearby. The building was an obvious attempt to impress visiting contestants. Hallway floors were made of inlaid marble blocks. A central stairway spiraled dramatically to the upper two stories, which held a large mess hall, a theater, and rooms for the *Pueblo* crew. Koreans occupied the first floor.

There were welcome changes for the crew in the new building. Here they were permitted to turn the lights off at night. There was better heat; the windows were uncovered; outdoor exercises were scheduled; and the beatings—though certainly programmed— were sporadic. If one were lucky, he might escape a blow indefinitely.

After the physical and psychological horror of the interrogations, the crew seemed to enjoy tempting fate for a bit of humor at their tormentor's expense. Almost invariably the fists and boots of irate guards would be generated, but Harris knew the thrill of getting back at them had helped bring the *Pueblo* team this far without emotional cracking.

He recalled the time the captain, marching the crew up the flight of stairs from the mess hall, was told by a guard—in Korean but with adequate gestures—to move them faster. "About face!" Bucher had called, feigning incomprehension. The men marched back downstairs to the obvious consternation of the guards. Inwardly delighted but posing seriousness, the crew followed their dangerous course until one of the men could not suppress a chuckle and received the butt of a submachine gun against his smirk.

Harris could not have catalogued the offenses, real or imagined by the guards, which were worthy of punishment even if he had had the heart for it. But there were nicer things to remember. The first mail from America was one of them. For six months the *Pueblo* crew had been presented very little truth about what was happening in the rest of the world. They were told, at various times: that the United States had sent a task force to the Sea of Japan and the battleship *New Jersey* had been sunk; that the U.S. had apologized for having intruded North Korean waters and, therefore, the crew would be sent home soon; that America was doing nothing and had forsaken them. Gradually Harris had been able to sift fact from fiction in the Korean reports, but initially it was hard to know what to believe. And that first mail call was a needed morale booster: the *Pueblo* had not been forgotten.

The mail had come in response to dictated letters the crew had written earlier. English-speaking Korean officers made sure that every letter home contained an admission of trespass by the *Pueblo* and a request that the American government apologize. Another lie the Koreans insisted on was that the writer was in good health and being treated well.

Every time he thought of this portion of the Korean dictation, Steve glanced down at his wasting frame. The condition of the crew worried him. Their bruises would heal in time, but as the days dragged by he wondered how much longer they could survive under the physical strain of an inadequate diet and the constant threat of torture.

At the brief group exercise period each morning he had witnessed the crew's deteriorating strength. Rosales had come down with some kind of sickness and was now too weak to get out of bed, but no medical attention was being given him. Harris himself, a husky 210-pound six-footer at the time of the capture, was to lose a fourth of his weight. Then there were the injured ones: the captain, Radioman Charley Crandell, Fireman Steve Woelk, Marine Sergeant Robert Chicca, and others with lesser shrapnel wounds.

Surprisingly, the crew's spirits remained high. It pleased Harris that the conduct of the communications technicians who served with him had contributed to the good morale.

There was Chief James Kell, who refused, even after eight months of captivity, to surrender his conviction that the crew would be released. His strange attitude of forgiveness toward the Korean captors was a puzzle to the embittered *Pueblo* sailors, but it had checked a dangerous course toward destructive self-pity. Even after his beatings Kell would pray for his tormentors, telling his roommates that the Koreans couldn't help themselves. "These people have had no chance to believe in God, no chance for a free society like we have in the United States," he would say. He had been a spiritual bolster to fellow Catholics who seemed to look to him for encouragement.

There was also CT Second-Class Joe Sterling, who was caught offering a blessing for the food. This had displeased the Korean officer on duty, who came to his table and demanded, "What are you doing?"

"Asking God to bless this food," Joe answered.

The officer pondered the reply a minute, then allowed Sterling to complete his meal. But afterward Joe was ordered into the hallway, where the duty officer and a second Korean officer asked him to repeat the prayer. It was a simple grace:

"Lord, we thank you for these blessings, and all of us ask for Christ's sake. Amen." It was a table blessing his father had taught him as a child.

"Say it again."

Sterling complied.

"What does *blessing* mean?" he was asked.

"It means"—he paused a second to think—"life, and wife, and

children, the air, the sun . . . and the food."

"Your food is a gift from the Korean people!" one of the officers instructed him. "But, very well. What does *sake* mean?"

"Well, it means getting God's forgiveness—"

"You are laughing stock! You make fool of yourself!" the other officer taunted. "Are you alone in this stupid ritual?"

Sterling hesitated. He knew most of the crew, many of whom had seldom done so before, were praying regularly and asking a blessing on the food. "Yes," he said carefully. "I'm the only one who offers this prayer."

Sterling was made to stand at attention for some time, then dismissed with an admonition not to pray in the future.

Sterling's treatment was unusually mild, but it pointed up an attitude about religion that the Koreans could not mask. They boasted that religion was permitted in their country, but every attempt at religious expression by the *Pueblo* crew was denied.

There was the cross that CT First-Class Don Peppard had carved from an ammunition box he'd found in the exercise yard. When it had been discovered, the guards fearfully kicked it around the room like an animal about to attack them. The knives which the men until then had been allowed to keep were taken away from them, and they were admonished to read the literature they had been given instead of carving.

Yet it seemed to Harris that the more the Koreans tried to take away the crewmen's faith, the more they moved in the direction of God. The men talked freely with each other about their prayers and their trust in God's help.

Although they were not permitted to have paper except for propaganda purposes, many of the crew wrote out Bible passages (the Twenty-third Psalm and John 3:16 were favorites) on scraps of paper and on toilet tissue which were passed around until finally they would be confiscated.

Because of his enforced confinement, Harris had little opportunity to share his faith, but in his room he had written out the

The Pueblo's six officers are shown in this photo taken by North Korean captors. Left to right are: Lt. J.G. Timothy Harris; Lt. J.G. F. Carl Schumacher, Jr.; Cdr. Lloyd Bucher; Lt. E. R. Murphy, Jr.; Lt. Stephen Harris; Chief Warrant Officer Gene H. Lacy.

Apostles' Creed, hymns, prayers, benedictions, and Bible verses. Particularly comforting to him were the verses giving assurance of salvation which he had learned shortly after his commitment to Christ. He wrote down the verses and the references as they returned to his mind:

> The wages of sin is death, but the free gift of God is eternal life in Christ Jesus our Lord. Romans 6:23.
>
> This is the testimony, that God gave us eternal life, and this life is in his Son. He who has the Son has life; he who has not the Son of God has not life. 1 John 5:11-12.
>
> All have sinned and fall short of the glory of God. Romans 3:23.

That last one was to help him keep from hating his captors.

On Sunday mornings Harris set apart a special time, in addition to his usual daily hour of prayer, during which he would silently observe every element of a worship service. In one attempt to share his faith he wrote out on a scrap of paper what it meant to be a Christian. He had carefully spelled out the trust one could put in God, who had revealed his love to undeserving man through his Son Jesus Christ, and how, by putting one's faith in him, a person could be happy on earth with the blessed expectation of living forever with God.

Just before the exercise period, the only time he could get a paper into the hands of a crewman, a guard had entered his room unexpectedly. Harris had tried to slip the paper into his pocket, but the action aroused the guard's suspicion. The lieutenant winced as he remembered how the guard had searched him. That morning he had traded all of the sacred scraps of paper for a collection of fresh bruises.

Harris knew he couldn't afford to dwell on his own troubles. He was worried about Pete. The captain had aged twenty years in their eight months of confinement, carrying on himself as he did the burden of the ship's capture and the plight of the men. Steve knew that many crewmen, as he, were praying daily for

Commander Bucher as well as for a rapid release.

But as day followed day and nothing seemed to change, he wondered if it might be God's purpose *not* to set them free. He and many of the men had put their trust in God as perhaps no other experience would have prompted them to do. And in spite of physical misery, Harris had found contentment in the inexplicable love of Christ. His reliance upon the divine will had at length become complete. Whatever happened would happen because God permitted it.

Harris reached for a piece of the Communist literature on the table. It was about time for dinner and he didn't want the guard to catch him daydreaming. He sat down and turned the pages slowly, his mind not fully registering what his eyes were reading. The stilted language was too reminiscent of the interrogator's harangue. For a second he relived the flying fists and boots. But there was no longer hate or fear. He knew now that God could erase memories too painful to recall.

3

THE BEAR

"Which one is Ginther?"

The North Korean officer was standing in the doorway of the room where Frank Ginther, Ramon Rosales, and Norman Spear were quartered.

Ginther's stomach knotted. *This is it.* He had felt this moment coming ever since Spear had hobbled back to the room a week ago, his face bruised, his stocky frame sagging, and collapsed into his bed. Rosales, too, had experienced Korean recompense. His Mexican-American features and short stature had led his captors to believe he was Oriental—a South Korean spy. The guards had addressed him in rapid Korean and answered his bewildered but naturally smiling countenance with hand chops and boot clips until he was finally able to convince English-speaking officers that he was not Korean—nor was his smile one of mockery. And now it was Ginther's turn. He stood up, keeping his chin tucked as he had been instructed to do in a gesture of submission. His thin blond hair tumbled lightly onto his forehead. He lowered his amber eyes.

"Follow me," the officer ordered. Ginther knew where the Korean would lead him. Knowing the destination was hardly reassuring, however. He had heard the groans and cries of pain coming from the interrogation room before.

In the room Ginther was confronted with three Korean officers, all sitting behind a table. None smiled. They motioned him to sit.

He did so on a wooden chair across the table from the Koreans. One of the officers, obviously the highest ranking for he did all the questioning, stood up and removed his belt. Ginther could see that it was made of thick leather with a bulky military buckle. He knew it was heavy when the officer pushed it to the table with a loud thump. Another officer was to be the interpreter. The third recorded the proceedings. The duty officer who had accompanied Ginther to the room joined the other Koreans.

Then through the interpreter the interrogation began. Ginther was asked to give his name, rank, and serial number. He realized soon enough that this was not what the Koreans were really interested in.

"What was *your* job, Mr. Ginther?"

"I'm a carpenter."

"Carpenter? Aboard the *Pueblo*?"

"Well, aboard the *Pueblo* I studied water."

"You studied water? No! *What was your job?*"

"I'm an oceanographer. I studied water."

There was a muttering in Korean. The interpreter spoke. "That is not a satisfactory answer. What was your specific duty aboard this *spy* ship?"

Determinedly, Ginther repeated his answer as the same question was asked again and again.

Suddenly, as if the thought had just occurred to him, the interrogator changed the question. "What was the course of your ship?"

Ginther hesitated. He had no idea. *What are they getting at?* "I don't know," he said.

The question was asked repeatedly with rising inflection and increasing consternation among the officers. "I really don't know," Ginther maintained. "I'm not a quartermaster. I had nothing to do with the navigation of the ship."

Question fell upon question. In one barrage Ginther's duties would be queried; in another, the course of the ship would be asked. The Koreans, as if in a wild self-hypnotism, were prodding themselves into a furor. They uttered contemptuous phrases in Korean. They banged on the table. Ginther could feel the pressure rising. His temples pulsated. His eyes began to sting and the ache piercing his forehead made the questions unintelligible. More frequently his answers became, "I don't understand."

The interrogator paused a moment, seemingly tired of the inquisition. Sweat beaded on Ginther's forehead. At length the officer picked up a paper in front of him. He spoke then, punctuating his speech with finger jabs at the paper as the interpreter carefully listed Ginther's statistics. "Francis John Ginther; born 20 June 1943 in Pottsville, Pennsylvania; height, five feet, ten inches; weight 188 pounds; dependents: wife and daughter living in Pottsville . . ." The Korean reviewed Ginther's Navy career— his previous assignments, his reenlistment, his intelligence training —and concluded with a frighteningly accurate description of his role in the communications detachment aboard the *Pueblo*. With a sickening feeling, Ginther realized the ship's personnel folders had been thoroughly studied. The Koreans knew everything. Coverup was futile. They had handed him his noose and he had tightened the knot.

"So *now*, are you ready to tell us the truth?" the interpreter finished.

Ginther was silent.

"You were in the territorial waters of the Democratic People's Republic of Korea!"

So that was what they wanted from him. "No!"

"You were in our waters!" Their dark eyes were blazing.

"I don't know."

"You were in our waters!"

Ginther's head was throbbing. He could not make the phrase possess meaning. "I don't understand."

As question followed question, exasperation mounted in his

tormentors. How long would they keep it up? Had he been here for hours? Or was it minutes that seemed like hours? How long before . . .

"Kneel down." The command did not immediately penetrate Ginther's fogged brain. "Kneel down!" Ginther sank to his knees. "Lift your chair above your head." Ginther took the legs of the heavy chair and raised it. "Over your head!" Ginther pushed the chair higher. "Hold it there."

A guard was called in. He stood beside the kneeling sailor, his submachine gun ready. The Korean officers seemed to relax, talking calmly among themselves but never looking away from the uplifted chair for more than a few seconds. Ginther knew what they were waiting for, and he wondered how long he would be able to keep the chair raised.

The pain started in the web of flesh between thumb and forefinger of Ginther's hands where the weight of the chair rested; it spread into his knuckles, swollen from his tense grasp; then traveled through his wrists, seared the muscles of his arms, inched across his shoulder blades, and cascaded down his spine into a whirlpool of agony in the small of his back. His knees ground into the rough floor and his toes numbed from his weight resting on them as he tried to keep the chair in position. At last, as he— and the waiting Koreans—knew he must, he relaxed his grip and the chair began its slow descent.

Ginther heard the gloat from the interrogator. The guard was ready. His heavy boot tore into Ginther's right arm. With a grunt Ginther lifted the chair, but now it was harder to hold because of the added pain in his arm. He had no idea how often he repeated the scene. Eventually the muscles would burst with pain, he would lose control of them, and the chair would drop. Automatically the boot would jab, sometimes into the arm, sometimes the ribs, sometimes the side of the head. More slowly and with greater effort each time, Ginther would lift the chair. On one attempt, when it had seemed impossible to lift again, Ginther muttered, "God! Please help me."

With an oath, the interrogator grabbed the belt from the table and whipped it across Ginther's face. As the buckle cracked against the sailor's temple, he heard a hollow pop as if from inside his skull. For a second everything was darkness, followed immediately by a fireworks' burst of brightness. In a defensive reflex movement, Ginther started to bring the chair down across the head of the interrogator, but checked the suicidal act. Through fuzzy eyes he could see the officers lunging at him, shouting something. Then he could hear the voices, and the sound reverberated inside his head. One of the officers was yelling in English, "Kill him! Kill him!" Another slapped him across the face with a ruler. The interrogator used the belt again. The guard was kicking, but it no longer mattered.

As Ginther slumped into semi-consciousness, the chair fell to the floor. The guard pulled the chair upright, yanked Ginther to his feet by the hair, and shoved him onto the chair. Ginther slumped; both sailor and chair fell to the side. A blow on the back of his head, instead of cancelling his last grasp of consciousness, momentarily cleared Ginther's mind. He heard the command to pick up his chair and sit down. He complied, and the questions started again.

"What was the course of the ship? What was the course of the ship? What was the course . . ."

"I don't know . . . I don't understand . . ."

Soon they were coming at him again. "Stop!" he cried.

A triumphant look crossed the face of the interrogator. He raised his eyebrows and spoke in Korean. "Are you ready to admit that the U.S.S. *Pueblo* trespassed our territorial waters?" the interpreter asked.

Ginther blinked hard, trying to clear his brain.

"Are you ready to confess that the *Pueblo* was in our territorial waters?" the interpreter was shouting.

That wouldn't be hard to admit, Ginther thought, since it was certainly in their waters now. But should he sign such a confession?

The interrogator studied Ginther's battered face. "I believe you are sorry now for your misdeeds," he said consolingly. "Confess that the *Pueblo* was in our territorial waters, and we'll let you go. We'll give you a lot of good food." Ginther thought of the last adequate meal the *Pueblo* crew had eaten, a turkey dinner a week before, on January 23.

"Confess!" The interrogator was in a rage again. "Admit it! You were in our territorial waters." Then, as if to add weight to the American guilt, he added, "And in Russian waters, too!"

The impossibility of being in two places at the same time didn't seem to bother the Koreans, but it pierced Ginther's numbed brain. The thought that was to occur to all of the interrogated Americans came to him then. He could make a patently false confession which would not stand up in an international court —especially since it would be made under duress—and *maybe* the beatings would stop. "Okay," he said hoarsely.

"You are ready to confess?"

"Yes."

Pottsville, Pennsylvania, is separated from Melrose, Massachusetts, by only a few hundred miles. But the cultural distance from the summit of Melrose's Boston Rock Road with its vista of metropolitan Boston to Pottsville's Hotel Street at the base of an Appalachian mountain would appear to be measurable only in light years. The man from Pottsville, unlike the man from Melrose, was not the son of a college instructor, nor a graduate of Harvard, nor the descendant of sea captains. He was, rather, the son of a milk delivery man, a product of Pennsylvania's anthracite coal-mining region, a career sailor who had enlisted in the Navy right after high school graduation at the age of seventeen.

Despite their disparate backgrounds, however, the men possessed a kindred sensitivity and empathic cordiality. A taste for light classical music could have given Pottsville's Frank Ginther common ground with Melrose's Steve Harris, Ginther's supervisor aboard the U.S.S. *Pueblo,* had there not been the Navy-honored separation of rank.

Officer and enlisted man could meet in the area of religion, however. Both Harris and Ginther had made commitments to the Christian faith. The lieutenant's decision had been made five years before in a simple home in Newport. Ginther's full assurance of salvation occurred in a detention barracks in Pyongyang, North Korea.

Not that Ginther had been unacquainted with the message of Christ. He had in fact been brought up in an atmosphere of conservative Protestantism in the Primitive Methodist Church of St. Clair, three miles from Pottsville. He had heard since infancy that Jesus loved him and had died for him. He had attended Sunday school regularly and memorized Bible verses. But he realized he didn't possess the strong convictions of his parents.

His mother had been a lifelong church member. He knew she prayed often for her son and daughter . . . and for her husband, a Catholic who had strayed from religious belief. The senior Francis Ginther had vowed he'd give his children a good father, but formal religion was not a part of the promise until his small son had urged, "Daddy, I want you to come to church, too." Frank had seen his father haltingly enter the ancient church building—the St. Clair parish was almost as old as American Methodism—and later hesitantly open a Bible for unaccustomed home study. He had witnessed the elder Ginther make a public profession of faith and grow into active membership in the small congregation. His mother's mother had been a spiritual force in his life, too. When Frank was a teenager she had been a Sunday school teacher in their church—and a notorious matchmaker. She had introduced Janice Scott of St. Clair, a bright-eyed brunette newcomer, to her grandson. Frank and Janice were married eighteen months after he joined the Navy, when both were nineteen.

Ginther posed for this Polaroid snapshot on deck of Pueblo shortly before the ship was captured.

His grandmother's death while they were in North Africa had been a blow to the young couple.

Religion became a decreasing influence in Frank's Navy life, however. There had been the excitement of travel—to California, Maryland, Morocco—and the birth of daughter Bonnie in 1965 to fill the sailor with a satisfactory sense of well-being. His transfer to the *Pueblo* had been taken in stride. As his first sea duty it would also mean the first lengthy separation for the pair, but while the ship was being outfitted in Bremerton, Washington, they could still be together.

Frank's introductory look at the *Pueblo* wasn't a reassuring one. The ship was tied to the dock, its hull scraped of paint and patched with primer, its superstructure encased with scaffoldings. The insistent machine-gun reverberation of air hammers against metal answered his salute to the colors and demanded a shouted request for permission to board. He wasn't at all sure the ridiculously small ship was seaworthy.

The bouncing Pacific crossing in the fall almost confirmed his initial dubiousness. The chow was good, however, and could have been a compensation for the cramped living and working areas if the crew hadn't been too seasick to enjoy it. A Thanksgiving turkey dinner on the way over was delicious. But he lost it.

In the Sea of Japan Ginther thought more and more about home. Janice and Bonnie were with his folks on Hotel Street in the house he had grown up in, one of many old homes that clung in rows to the mountainside. Above the houses were the woods that he had visited so often as a child. It was probably just the uneasiness of being halfway around the world from his family that caused it, Frank told himself, but he felt an ominous uncertainty. He wondered if he would ever see them again. In his locker was a Bible that he had not looked at for some time. He got it out and started reading.

Perhaps the only *Pueblo* crewman to know the time of the captured ship's arrival in Wonsan harbor was Frank Ginther. He had been blindfolded as had all the others, but the cloth had been placed high on his forehead. He could see beneath it and watched the minutes pass silently by on his electric Timex. It was 6:30 when the ship crushed against the wharf. The sun was down when he stepped out of the compartment where the crew had been held. Lights on the pier illuminated the *Pueblo's* decks as the Americans were searched and their hands tied. Ginther was able to see the deck immediately in front of him and the narrow plank that connected the *Pueblo* with North Korea. With suspicious smoothness he followed the push of the Korean guards lining the route to captivity, while fellow crewmen stumbled around him. A guard discovered the raised blindfold then and struck a sharp back-handed blow across Ginther's face. The Korean pulled the blindfold down and grabbed the sailor's watchcap, stretching it over his head. The next opportunity Ginther had to look at his watch came after the night's train ride, when the crew was unbound for the propaganda photos. It was 6:00 A.M.

The days which immediately followed were the longest. Hope of some kind of U. S. reaction died slowly. The interrogations hadn't yet given the crewmen something else to occupy their minds. As in the other rooms, the hushed conversation in the one occupied by Rosales, Spear, and Ginther centered around the possibility of American retaliation.

"You think they're going to do anything?" Rosales asked.

"Not now," Spear answered, his discouragement unmasked. "They should have done something while we were still on the water. It's too late now. They'll just let us rot here."

"Aw, I don't think they've forgotten us," Ginther interrupted. "But I don't think they're going to do anything that might start another war." He felt a responsibility as a senior petty officer to avoid pessimism. But he could muster little optimism himself.

"So how long does it take them to do something?" Spear asked.

"It won't happen right away, I'm sure of that" Ginther said. He had heard that the North Koreans kept prisoners for an average of two years, but he didn't want to share this information. "The Koreans are going to wring all the propaganda they can out of this before they release us," he said.

"You know what I wish?" Rosales broke in. "I don't care if they kill us all—I just hope the U.S. drops a bomb on this stupid country—" Footsteps near the door silenced the conversation. Rosales inhaled deeply. Had he been overheard? The steps went on by.

The men waited a minute after the guard had passed. "You really wouldn't mind if they killed us?" Ginther broke the silence.

"No!" Rosales answered. "I'd go to heaven . . . I think." He paused, as if considering the possibility now for the first time. Then he added, "I know my mother would be praying for me . . . and my father . . . and my eleven brothers and sisters . . . and the fathers at St. Anthony's Seminary in El Paso . . . . That's a lot of prayers."

"I've been doing a lot of praying myself lately," Ginther said.

"You too?" Spear asked.

"I sure have." He thought of the capture and how he had dived for the deck and prayed for deliverance when the Koreans opened fire. There had been other prayers since then, resulting in an experience he was anxious to share, but he didn't know if his Catholic roommates would understand his Protestant terminology. "I've been thinking quite a bit lately about the Bible's promise of everlasting life," he tried.

Both Spear and Rosales nodded. He took it as a signal to continue. But how to form the message? He wanted to use the right words to tell them why he thought God had brought them this far and why he was confident of the future. At first he had had trouble making Hodges' death fit into the picture, but he knew the retiring fireman was acquainted with God. Certain things you learned on a ship as small as the *Pueblo*.

"I was thinking," he began, "how almost anything could have gone wrong on that day we were captured. You know, with the firing by the Koreans and the burning we were doing, it's a wonder we weren't sunk or all killed. But we weren't and . . . well, if we survived that day, we've got a lot to thank God for." The others were still listening. "I wasn't real sure of my salvation before our capture, you know? But ever since, I've been remembering God's promises in the Bible. Well, you know them."

He quoted John 3:16. " 'God so loved the world that he gave his only begotten Son that whosoever believeth in him should not perish but have everlasting life.' I asked myself, 'If we'd all been killed that day, would I have been ready to receive everlasting life?' I decided I wasn't quite as ready as I should be."

He paused, hoping to get the right words now, for this was important. "Another Bible verse came to me. I read it just the night before they took us. It's the one where Jesus says, 'I am the way, the truth, and the life. No man cometh to the Father but by me.' That one really got to me. Here he was offering me salvation and I had just ignored it. I asked God to forgive me for drifting away from him. And, you know, he *did* it."

Ginther shook his head then at the wonder of it. "I can't tell you how I know, but—he just gave me the assurance. I know now that God is right here with us. I don't care if they put me in a *box,* they'll never take God away from me."

"That's for sure," Rosales agreed.

"Yeah—" Spear began, but he didn't finish his thought. A Korean woman was bringing them their food. It was dangerous to be caught talking about such things.

The promised good treatment did not follow the forced confessions, which were made more ignominious by their propaganda exploitation in press and television. The guards and duty officers seemed as eager as ever to exact immediate punishment for imagined offenses. They delighted in alternately dangling threats and promises before their captives. For the crewmen, never knowing what to expect was worse than a definite sentence of execution. But uncertainty within the opponent was the object of the diabolic game.

Not long after the confessions, the Americans were instructed to give their quarters a thorough cleaning. Spear and Ginther were ordered to take care of the captain's room. Their entry caught Commander Bucher by surprise. "What's going on?" he asked.

"We don't know, sir," Ginther replied. "We were just told to come and clean your room. Didn't you know anything about it?"

"No."

As they worked, Ginther stole glances at his commander. It was the first time he had seen him at close range since the crew had been forced to sign a joint letter to the U. S. government early in their captivity. The sailors were appalled at the captain's gaunt appearance.

After the barracks clean-up the Americans were loaded onto buses for their mysterious covered-window ride to the second building on Pyongyang's outskirts.

The enlisted men's new rooms were larger than the rooms in the Barn, but this only meant more prisoners would be in them. Ginther, Rosales, and Spear were placed in room 3-8 along with five other men. The consignment included a mixture of nationalities and religious affiliations. There were three Filipinos: Storekeeper Policarpo Garcia and Stewards Rogelio Abelon and Rizalino Aluague; a Mexican-American to join Rosales, Yeoman Armando Canales; and Fireman Tom Massie. The Spanish names should have been giveaways for Catholic backgrounds, which was true of most, but Abelon was a Protestant and Garcia a Mason. Massie was a Baptist. Their experiences of God's helpfulness were to transcend denominational labels, however.

As in the Barn, there was a bed and chair for each man. In addition, the room contained nightstands for each, a round table big enough to seat all eight occupants, a large closet, and a mirror. Unlike the Barn's single, bald lightbulb, the new room had two globed light fixtures. But, like the Barn, the floorboards in the new sleeping quarters were warped and separated, a characteristic, apparently, of Korean construction.

Except for the unpredictable beatings, a routine was soon established. Two exercise periods were held each day—one in the morning with the officers and another in the afternoon. When they were not in the four-hour, twice-weekly indoctrination meetings attended by a third of the crew at a time, the men were supposed to study the literature with which they had been so generously supplied. Playing cards and chess sets were provided for evening recreation, but the time was often spent in guarded conversation. Saturdays meant general clean-up. Sunday was a day of rest.

For a while Ginther checked the routine with his watch. Then the energy cell died and he set the time permanently at twelve o'clock, deciding for some reason that it looked best at that hour. The inability to time the boredom represented no great deprivation, however. The lengthy lectures and the voluminous literature were filled with oft-repeated anti-Americanisms. The nation seemed to be raised on hate. One of the men counted the phrase "U.S. imperialist" over a hundred times in one magazine. The intelligence crewmen who could speak Korean were able to catch the same diatribe floating from the loud-speakers in the nearby village. In the Korean movies which were shown once a week, the manipulation of minds could be seen even before the film's interpretation by the duty officer. The hero was always pushing his production in the people's factory or following in the footsteps of the glorious liberators who had driven the American aggressors from the land. A child in the picture might be asked, "What do you want to do when you grow up?" The reply would be "Kill an American!" A children's stage production in Pyongyang that the *Pueblo* crew had to attend included a dance in which the youngsters aimed guns at an actor dressed as a U. S. soldier.

Almost everything the crew observed—the movies and stage

plays they attended; the newspapers and magazines they read; the television they were shown once, on the twentieth anniversary of the Democratic People's Republic in October; or the loud-speakers they could hear blaring incessantly at the villagers—revealed the total control the Korean government held over the lives and minds of the people. They could readily believe the officers who advised them not to attempt to escape because the citizens would destroy them.

And they could understand why the guards and duty officers treated them as they did. Not that all were monsters, but it seemed that just when some of the Koreans began to realize their American captives were fellow human beings, they would be replaced by other guards possessing a more retaliatory nature.

The Bear, however, who was with them from April to July, never seemed to lose his hostility. Because the guards could not speak English, the Americans identified each with an uncomplimentary label. There was "Little Caesar," "Blockhead," and "Fly." The officers, too, were labeled—"Frogface," "Snake," "Dum-Dum," and "The Glorious General"—but not so openly, especially if they could speak English. The interpreters were given names like "Wheezy," "Silverlips," "Captain Nice," and "Highpockets."

The Bear earned many nicknames from the crew. At first he was called the Halfbreed because his height and complexion indicated some Caucasian ancestry. Later the men in 3-8 referred to him as Gooney Bird because he reminded one of them of the birds that inhabit Midway Island. Other appellations were even less complimentary. But the one name that satisfied the entire crew because of the guard's massive build and aggressive nature was "The Bear." At six feet he towered above his fellow Koreans and really didn't need the ever-present submachine gun, which the other guards relied on so heavily, to make his authority believable.

He was forever suspicious. Unashamedly he would peek through keyholes to see if he could catch a crewman napping or departing from the literature study. He believed in prompt punishment and dealt it brutally with thick hand or heavy boot. A strict disciplinarian, he had no favorites. The Americans respected his presence when he reported to the third-floor hallway for his two-hour guard duty three times a day.

The Bear was in the hallway the day Spear's belt broke when he was returning from ,the bathroom. Spear quickly grabbed his trousers; he had lost so much weight on the Korean diet that he needed the belt. The embarrassed look on Spear's face aroused the Bear's suspicion. He followed the sailor to 3-8 and entered behind him. With rapid speech and hand gestures the Korean wanted to know what Spear was trying to hide.

"Well, my belt broke," the American explained, still holding onto his pants. The Bear chopped Spear on the side of the head with one meaty hand and took a firm grasp on his shirt with the other. Terrified, Spear still clung to the pants. The Bear shook him roughly and thrust a boot into his shins.

The other Americans, standing around or sitting at the table, no longer pretended to be reading. "Show him your broken belt," Ginther suggested. This infuriated the Bear, who lunged at Ginther with the wildly pawing blows that had earned him his nickname.

Later Spear and Ginther were called into the galley for clean-up, a favorite punishment duty dispensed by the Korean officers. The kitchen was also a favored retreat for the administration of punitive beatings. The two worked silently scrubbing the floor until Ginther was told abruptly that he was dismissed. He returned to 3-8, followed later by Spear, who was doubled up in pain. He was gasping and speechless, but it was obvious that he had received a popular Korean revenge—a crushing kick in the groins.

The crewmen despaired of anticipating the actions of the sadistic Bear. Nothing could please him, except the meting out of punishment. Nor was he easily convinced that an American had "repented" of his wrongdoing. Some of the men discovered that he found fault most often with whoever might be sitting in the chair opposite the door. They could never prevent the Bear's punishment of the hapless individual in that particular chair, but they were able to make the situation equitable. They rotated their positions around the table.

The Bear was but one in a seemingly unending line of perplexities the harried Americans were facing. There was increasing doubt in Ginther's mind about the prospects of getting out. Yet he felt a strange calm. While he continued to pray daily for release, he asked as well for daily strength. He found that the mere knowledge of God's presence could see him through every day, the Bear notwithstanding.

Most of the crew were learning, too, that when there was nowhere else to turn for help, they could turn to God. Spiritual discussions became common. Prayer became routine. Familiar Bible passages were brought to mind. Ginther wrote out the Twenty-third Psalm, John 3:16, the Apostles' Creed, and the Lord's Prayer on scraps of paper which he put inside his nightstand. He referred to them frequently until he came back from exercise period one day and discovered they had been taken.

As the Koreans uncovered the papers, punishment increased. When it became too dangerous to possess them, the passages—committed to memory—were recited back and forth.

Mail from home helped then. One letter Ginther received from Janice was filled with Bible verses. They raised his own sagging spirit so much, he chanced sharing them with others.

The verses were discovered on Radioman Lee Hayes. "What are these?" the duty officer demanded.

"Why, just some quotes," Hayes stammered.

"What good are they?"

"I find them comforting."

"Did you write them?"

Hayes considered the test he faced. If he were to tell the

source, he knew that Ginther would be punished. If he concealed it, *he* would be in trouble. "They're mine," he answered slowly. It was worth risking the bruises not to jeopardize the mail receipt; letters from home were a vital factor in making the imprisonment bearable.

On the envelope of one letter Janice had written, "Attention Korea: Please let my husband have this letter. He has a family." Ginther was surprised the letter got through, but he was glad it did. Inside she had printed in bold letters: "And nobody can break me down, for I have the Holy Spirit living within me." Tears came to Ginther's eyes. What a powerful thought. Then it hit him: That was why he had been able to look into the bleak future with confidence. He had God living right inside him. The knowledge was to help him through the discouraging days ahead.

"Do you think God wants us all to die?" Abelon asked one evening when everyone but he and Ginther had gone to the bathroom.

"What's the matter with you, Rogelio?" Ginther asked.

"Sometimes I think God doesn't hear our prayers. Almost everyone of us has been praying, and our families are praying, and here we sit."

"God hears us all right," Ginther told him. "When things get tough, it's easy to blame God, but that's just when we've got to trust him the most. You just keep praying and believing that God will help us, and we'll get out of here." Ginther was surprised at his own aplomb. Defense of the faith was a new experience for him. He didn't know he was soon to engage in it again—with his captors.

The crew had been able to sit impassively through the anti-American harangue of the indoctrination lectures with its usual lack of respect for their knowledge. (Did the Koreans really expect them to believe that America imported their lightbulbs; or that the flies which swarmed the place—called the "national bird of Korea" by the crew—had been placed there by U.S.

biological warfare; or that the North Koreans would "peacefully" unify Korea if America would leave?) But then the indoctrination wandered into the area of religion.

"Missionaries are spies who carry secret messages in their Bibles," the lecturer told them. "Every cross on their churches is a radio transmitter sending intelligence information to their homeland." A movie showed a priest sicking his dog onto a child. Another showed a missionary branding a small boy on the forehead with the word "thief" for stealing an apple. At the end of the session, the officer asked for questions. There was silence, but obvious consternation among the crew. "The Russians explored space and couldn't find God," the officer bantered. "Where is he?" The Americans fidgeted but remained silent. "We dug holes all over the place and never found hell," the lecturer said. "Where is it?" There was no reply.

"Most of you are Christians," the officer went on. "What a stupid religion! How can you explain the birth of Christ? It is scientifically impossible for a child to be born of a virgin. You are all grown men. You surely know that! How could you be taken in by such a myth?"

This was too much. " 'With God all things are possible,' " a crewman quoted. "Anyway, it is a recorded historical fact. People who witnessed Jesus' life wrote down what they saw themselves and what they were told by eyewitnesses."

"And you believe this? You people are told so much untruth, you don't know what to believe." This statement amused the Americans. "And how could a man come alive again after he is dead? Surely you must know that no one comes back to life after death."

"Well, this too is recorded," the sailor answered. "But how can we explain something supernatural, something only God could do, to you when you refuse to accept the fact that there is a God?"

"I have never seen God," the Korean replied. "Of course, I don't believe in him. Have *you* seen God? Has he ever spoken to you? What does he look like? Is he fat or thin? Is he short or tall? Could you show me his picture?"

"Sure, we've seen God," another sailor interposed. "We see him in the trees he's made, in the flowers. We hear him in the song of the bird."

The Korean only laughed.

Ginther spoke then. "Maybe you can't understand, or won't accept, the fact that Jesus Christ was born of a virgin and that he died for your sins and rose from the dead. Okay. The important thing is what you do about your beliefs. Look at us. Are we really American imperialist devils? We believe the Bible. With God's help we're able to follow its teachings. Don't steal. Don't kill. Love your enemies."

The Korean didn't answer immediately. When he did, he agreed these were indeed worthy goals. But he was committed to other ideals; the discussion soon ended.

In the fall, when Rosales took sick and couldn't seem to get well, the plight of the *Pueblo* crew was brought home to the men in 3-8. Insidiously, their bodies had grown weaker. It took longer and longer to overcome even simple illnesses. The lack of proper food had taken its toll. Where beatings had failed to crush their spirit, the debilitating diet threatened to subdue them.

Not only had the amount of food been insufficient; the crew had often been fearful of eating it. The butchered pork and trucked-in fish were piled in the open yard outside the whitewashed building, attracting swarms of Korea's "national bird" as it rotted. It was served until consumed.

Almost every crewman was now praying for a release before it was too late. But, just as the expectation of American assistance on the day of capture had faded with the waning sunlight, hope for the repatriation of the *Pueblo* crew was slowly dissolving.

4

"REMEMBER THE PUEBLO"

She turned her head on the pillow and was opening her eyes to the early January morning when she saw him. He was in his dress blues, staring at her, a troubled look on his face. She tried to call his name, but it came out a whisper. "Steve." She reached out for him, but the figure dissolved.

Esther Harris sat up in her bed. She suppressed an impulse to run to her mother. It was only 7:30 and the older woman, recuperating from a leg amputation of the previous October, needed her rest.

"Is Steve in trouble?" she wondered half-aloud. She put on her slippers and robe and walked to the window. The sun was just rising over the snow-covered Montreal landscape.

He had seemed so real standing there. What did it mean? *Was* Steve in trouble? In her mind she went back to the time in Naselle, Washington, when she was eight years old. She had had a vision then, too, and it had been just as real. Christ, with two angels, had suddenly appeared before her. Jesus seemed to beckon to her, and without really considering what to do, she had gone to the altar of her father's church. There, in faltering words, she had told the Savior of her desire to give her heart to him. And now, with the image of her troubled husband in her mind, there was only one thing to do. She returned to the bed to kneel and pray.

Her parents had enough to worry about, Esther decided, so she did not tell them about the vision. The memory of Steve's strange appearance stayed with her, however, and she prayed more frequently for him.

Near the end of the month, when her mother seemed better, Esther paid a visit to brother Gus in Washington, D.C. It was good returning to the place where she had met Steve. But her joy soon melted. On the twenty-second her father called to say that her mother had suffered a stroke and was paralyzed. Esther decided to return to Montreal.

First she phoned Steve's mother, who had also been ill. She learned that Mrs. Harris was returning to her teaching the next day, the three-week recuperation after a severe case of flu over at last.

The fourth graders of Decius Beebe School wildly greeted Mrs. Eleanor Harris's return to class. She enjoyed pitting her five-foot-two frame against the challenges of her "cherubs." The morning went well, but by noon she felt uneasy. She wondered what could be causing her nervousness. Had she returned to work too soon? At lunch another teacher asked about Steve.

"He's fine, I guess," she answered, cheered by the introduction of her favorite subject. "Way off on sea duty somewhere. He phoned me from Japan during the Sasebo rioting. Afraid I'd be worried. He's such a wonderful guy."

The afternoon of her return to teaching proved increasingly disturbing, both mentally and physically, for Mrs. Harris; and she was given permission to leave when the children did.

At the "Ledgewinds" signpost she turned her Volkswagen off Boston Rock Road onto the uphill drive and chugged into the garage of the house that crowned the hill. She sank into an easy chair right after hanging up her coat, stretched her weary limbs, and closed her eyes. The telephone jangled as she did so, but she let it ring, reluctant to leave the restful spot. At last she forced herself to satisfy the demanding instrument. "Hello."

"Mrs. Harris?"

"Yes."

"I'm calling from the headquarters of the First Naval District in Boston," a man's restrained voice said. "We have just received a telegram from naval headquarters in Washington. Please listen carefully. The U.S.S. *Pueblo*, to which your son is attached, has been boarded by the North Korean military while in international waters and has been towed into Wonsan harbor." He paused. Mrs. Harris was silent, trying to put meaning into the words. "When we have further details," the voice concluded, "we will notify you."

She asked the poignant questions which flooded her mind, but there was nothing more the man could tell her. Finally she whispered a thank you and returned the handpiece to its hook.

First my husband, she thought, *and now my only son.*

Steve's wife was reached with the same message at her brother's home in Washington. "What should I do?" she asked Gus. "I need to be in Montreal with Mother, but I want to be close to Washington, too, in case there's any word about Steve." There was a prayer for guidance and for Steve's safety. Then the decision was made for Esther to go to Montreal until her mother was better, when she would return to Washington.

Through the day other wives and mothers received the Navy's limited information. Some, however, got the word ahead of the telephoned message. In Pottsville, Pennsylvania, that morning Janice Ginther had overslept. It was almost ten o'clock before she had forced herself from under the warm covers. She was dressing two-year-old Bonnie in the living room of the Ginther home when the phone rang.

Phyllis Smith, a Navy wife Janice had met in Bremerton, Washington, was on the line. After the preliminaries of identification and Janice's surprise at the call from Maryland, Phyllis asked, "Have you heard from Frank?"

"I just got a letter," Janice answered. "He'll be home next month."

There was a pause. "Janice, that's not what I'm talking about.

Haven't they told you what happened? I mean, to his ship?"

"No . . . what?"

"I just heard a radio report about the *Pueblo*. It had something to do with the Communists, but I didn't catch it all. I thought I'd give you a ring. Better turn on the news. . . ."

Janice thanked her and twisted the radio knob. Music, commercials, weather—but no news. She located the number of Pottsville's station WPPA in the directory and dialed. The radio station personnel could only give her fragments of information which they had received from their press services: a U.S. ship had been captured off the coast of North Korea.

Just the day before, Janice recalled then, she had felt strangely depressed. She hadn't been able to put a finger on what might have been causing it, but she'd wondered if Frank was all right. Janice prayed again now for his welfare. The radio gave its hourly report on the news; there still seemed to be no certain word on the identity of the captured vessel. At noon she turned on the TV set—and stared at the picture of her husband's ship. She learned then that it was the *Pueblo* that had been boarded off the North Korean coast and taken into Wonsan Harbor. The Navy reached her with the information that afternoon.

The news had gotten to her reasonably fast at that. Not many hours earlier, as most of America slept, communications technicians at the Yokosuka headquarters of the Commander of U. S. Naval Forces in Japan had begun to realize something out of the ordinary was happening. Unusual teletype messages were coming in from the *Pueblo*.

Soon commands were being issued; messengers were scurrying; dispatches were going out over other machines. "Have been directed to come to all stop and being boarded," the *Pueblo's* message now read. "Got four men injured, one critically." The officers and men around the machine admired the coolness of the operator aboard the *Pueblo*.

Then: "Going off the air now and destroying this gear." The clacking stopped.

There was an exchange of worried glances and a quick command. "Can you transmit?" went out the message to the *Pueblo*.

Silence.

"Can you transmit?"

There was no reply.

It couldn't have happened. Even after rereading the teletype transmission of the capture, it was almost impossible to believe. The U.S.S. *Banner,* the *Pueblo's* predecessor in the surveillance of the Sea of Japan, had at one time been surrounded and harassed by eleven Communist P-4s, but without being fired upon or boarded. On January 9 the North Korean government had radioed a charge that American spy ships were operating off Korea, and warned that the Koreans were prepared to take action. The broadcast was just one of many such warnings, however. Although it was received by the Defense Intelligence Agency in Washington and published the next day in the file of foreign broadcasts issued by the Foreign Broadcast Information Service, no defensive operation was formulated; for there had been no real concern. Even the two destroyers that formerly accompanied such surveillance missions had been transferred from the area. It was felt they represented a provocative element, and any appearance of provocation was being meticulously avoided.

But now it was time for action. One of the first acts was to protect the code system which might have been compromised with the *Pueblo* capture. Within an hour all U. S. naval ships and stations around the world were ordered to stop using the current ciphers.

The Commander of the Naval Forces in Japan, Rear Admiral Frank L. Johnson, still faced a nightmarish decision with a prize intelligence vessel and eighty-three lives at stake. *Where* would he get assistance for the *Pueblo*? The nearest naval aircraft was on the nuclear carrier *Enterprise* 600 miles away. He turned to the Commander of the U. S. Forces in Japan, Air Force Lieutenant General Seth J. McKee, who also headed the Fifth Air Force.

General McKee was frustrated, too. Barely fifteen minutes flying time the Koreans could get the *Pueblo* into harbor. Four more were four U. S. fighter planes, but one was out of commission and the other three were armed with nuclear weapons. It would have taken up to three hours to shift to conventional arms. By that time the Koreans could get the *Pueblo* into harbor. Four more planes were landing at the airfield that day—all had nuclear arms.

McKee did the next best thing. He ordered F-105s, armed with 20-mm cannon, from Okinawa. That was 900 miles away, but they were the only operationally ready combat units available. They had to stop at Osan for refueling. Darkness engulfed the Sea of Japan before they could reach the captive *Pueblo*.

In Washington, fourteen hours behind Korean time, news of the *Pueblo's* capture arrived just before midnight. Reports on the attack were distributed simultaneously to the State Department's Operations Center, the Pentagon's National Military Command Center, and the Situation Room in the White House. Defense Secretary McNamara was alerted at 12:23 A.M. At 12:45 President Johnson's national security affairs officer, Walter Rostow, who had also been advised, drove to the White House, arriving at 1:15 A.M. Shortly after two o'clock he telephoned the President, who stayed in bed but was briefed during the next four hours as details became known. The President immediately conferred by telephone with Secretary of State Dean Rusk and with McNamara, and instructed Rostow to prepare an intelligence report. The report was completed by seven o'clock and placed on Mr. Johnson's breakfast tray.

The hijack was evidently well planned. A possible ambush awaited any rescue force: fifty to a hundred MIGs were perched at Wonsan, and South Korean intelligence had spotted two additional Communist squadrons flying near the demilitarized zone at the time of the *Pueblo's* capture. By the time the intelligence information reached the President, further conventional rescue attempts were considered hopeless. The *Pueblo* had probably already reached Wonsan harbor; darkness prevented air rescue.

Admiral John J. Hyland, Commander of the U.S. Pacific Fleet, didn't want to give up yet. He dispatched a destroyer toward North Korea with the "possible mission" of sailing into Wonsan harbor, recapturing the *Pueblo,* and towing it back to a U.S. base. At the same time the *Enterprise* and its escorting frigate *Truxtun* were ordered to head for the area.

The orders were countermanded, however. The rescue operation was started too late. Deflating as the realization was, it had to be recognized that one of the world's foremost military powers did not have the retaliatory capacity ready in the right place to come to the aid of one of its team members. The President's chief concern, as a result, was what to do now to regain the ship and crew without endangering the men's lives. Complicating his decision was the danger of renewing the Korean war, forcing America to defend a second front on the Asian mainland.

Johnson immediately called on Korean truce negotiators in Panmunjom to begin talks on the release of the crew. The next day he ordered 14,787 Air Force and Navy reservists to duty. In the wake of the reserve call-up, aides of Russian Premier Alexi Kosygin hinted that perhaps the U.S. could get the *Pueblo* and its crew back by paying a fat fine, as Russian trawlers had been forced to do after being apprehended within U.S. territorial limits off Alaska in March of 1967.

In its report of the capture the North Korean news agency claimed that forces of the Democratic People's Republic had fired on the *Pueblo* only after the American ship had first fired. The Navy teletype records, however, clearly indicated that Commander Bucher had not offered resistance, in compliance with his own previous orders. The U.S. State Department issued a prompt denial of the North Korean charge.

American and world leaders were soon voicing their reactions to the incident. Utah's Republican Senator Wallace Bennett urged the U.S. to send "an armada steaming into Wonsan harbor, throw a tow rope around the *Pueblo,* and get her out of there." Presidential candidate Richard Nixon called the affair a "tactical blunder." South Korean Premier Chung Il Kwon urged massive retaliation, warning that "a lukewarm U.S. response would encourage the Communists to engage in another Korean war."

On January 25 the carrier *Enterprise* and three escort cruisers were sent to the Sea of Japan to maneuver off the North Korean coast. Shadowing the *Enterprise,* sometimes coming as close as 800 yards, was the Soviet trawler *Gidrolog,* a spy ship probably as loaded with electronic gear as the *Pueblo.*

The next day North Korea declared itself fully combat ready and promised an "exterminatory blow" at the United States if North Korea were attacked. On nationwide television that evening President Johnson told the American people that North Korea had committed "another wanton and aggressive act" and that the U.S. was presenting the issue to the United Nations Security Council. He urged the people to "exhibit in this crisis, as they have in other crises, determination and unity, which is necessary to see it through."

On January 30 the Defense Department reported the death of one of the *Pueblo* crewmen, and American concern was intensified. How crazy were the North Koreans anyway? Were other Americans seriously wounded? *Whose* son or husband had been killed? One question was answered on February 7.

Jesse and Stella Hodges were, uncharacteristically, both awake at 5:00 A.M. when a Navy petty officer knocked on their door. Both answered the knock; both knew what the man had come to tell them. Despite the official word that it was their son Duane who had been killed during the *Pueblo* capture, they continued to pray for the release of the crewmen—and to hold onto a slim hope that there might have been a mistake.

Many Americans joined the friends and relatives who were praying for the *Pueblo* crew as it became apparent their detention might drag on for some time. They showed their concern in other ways as well.

Mrs. Eleanor Harris had always enjoyed entertaining; her rambling hilltop home was often filled with guests. But not even her open houses could compare with the constant procession of friends, clergymen, Navy men, newsmen, and cameramen who streamed through her doors when it was learned that one of the captured *Pueblo* crewmen was from Boston.

Not every visitor was altruistically motivated. On a brisk evening in late January Mrs. Harris came home from school to find broken dishes on the floor, cabinets yawning open, shelves disarranged, and the beds and floors littered with costume jewelry, papers, and nylons. The back door was open. She wondered if the vandals had made a quick exit or if they were now upstairs. Closing the door, she noticed with dismay the jagged hole in the picture window that framed downtown Boston. Through glazed eyes, she looked around, hoping to form a word description before she called the police. Burglary was not attempted, she was sure: she recognized familiar valuables in the jumble. A tape recorder she had been using that morning to prepare a message to her daughter-in-law was still on the kitchen table.

She put her hand on the telephone, to be startled by its ring. Before she could say anything the voice of a neighbor came through the receiver. "Eleanor! Steve's alive! I heard him on the radio just now. He's making some sort of a confession."

"Alive! What station? A confession?"

Whether the house had been ransacked by vandals, a frustrated thief, or by more sinister intruders neither Mrs. Harris nor the Melrose police ever learned. But right then she had to get to the radio. She turned the dial until she found the station carrying the recording. Doctored and ludicrous as the message sounded, she tried to make the tired, strained voice sound like her son's.

It was the only contact she was to have with him until March, when she received a letter addressed to Esther and herself. The two were overjoyed to hear from Steve, but portions of the letter were disturbing . . .

> Don't worry about me, because I am being treated well by the Korean people. It is no news by now that the *Pueblo* was captured in the act of collecting intelligence in the territorial waters of the Democratic People's Republic of Korea. The penalty for espionage in this country is death. The only condition that we will be returned home on is for the U.S. government to admit its crime, apologize and give assurance that it will not happen again. If these conditions are not met, then we will be executed for the acts. I love you both so much that even as a grown man I have broken into tears many times.
>
> With all my love,
Stephen Robert Harris

It was one of many similar letters sent by the crewmen to loved ones and government officials. The appeal for a U.S. apology was a puzzle to all. It seemed, very obviously, a Korean dictation; but in every one of Steve's letters were some acceptable facts. In a later letter he wrote:

> . . . Although I am detained here, the Lord never fails to give continuing comfort. My faith never wavers; it's only stronger than it has ever been. I am certain I shall return, but God works through your efforts, so use them wisely and implement them positively in order that we may be returned.

Some of the crewmen's letters hinted at the Korean subterfuge by oblique references to nonexistent objects or "greetings to Uncle George" (dead a dozen years). One contained the comment that the North Korean captors were gentle people, the nicest the writer had seen since his last visit to St. Elizabeth's (a U.S. mental hospital in Washington, D.C.). But other phrases were difficult to decode, gray areas that left readers gnawingly in doubt.

In every letter the crewmen, always repeating their pleas for an apology, seemed overly insistent that they were receiving humane treatment: eating three nourishing meals a day, getting medical checkups, enjoying outdoor exercise, and seeing Korean mov-

Harris sent this photo taken by the North Koreans to his wife and mother. They could tell he had lost a lot of weight.

ies. But the thinness Steve displayed in a photograph included in one letter bothered both Mrs. Harris and Esther.

In Pottsville the Ginthers were perplexed by portions of Frank's letters that were so unlike him in language and thought.

> I don't want you to worry about me as we are all being treated well. We are living in a clean modern building and have been supplied with all the necessities for our daily living. We are given three meals a day and we are allowed to exercise by playing volleyball, basketball and various other sports. We are shown movies and also allowed to play cards in the evenings. By this you can see we are being treated well.

Was he carefully reciting facts or was he concerned lest the real truth about his condition be too distressing? He had never played cards. They read on.

> As you know, we are prisoners of the Democratic People's Republic of Korea. We are charged with committing espionage and invading their territorial waters. This is a very serious offense and we can be dealt with severely. The DPRK is treating us leniently and with human understanding.

> Let me explain the facts to you. We were captured when deep within their territorial waters conducting espionage. We violated their territorial waters several times. This, along with the charges of espionage, is true. During our capture we tried to destroy all our equipment and documents, but time was insufficient to complete the job. As a result some of the secret and top secret documents were captured by the Korean People's army. The documents and navigational charts and logs, plus the frank and sincere confessions of the officers and men, prove we are guilty of committing espionage deep within the territorial waters.

> At first I denied it, but I could no longer deny it after seeing the evidence and hearing the confessions of the captain, executive officer, research officer, and operations officer. We now have the U.S. denial that we of the U.S.S. *Pueblo* were conducting espionage in the territorial waters of the DPRK. This is a very foolish move because it jeopardizes our fate and future. But it is proven conclusively and undeniably through the evidence captured that we are guilty as charged.

> Hopefully I will return home, but it is in jeopardy because of the denials and attitude taken by the U.S. government. The U.S. must admit that we conducted espionage within the territorial waters of the DPRK. It must apologize to the DPRK and guar-

antee that the hostile acts of espionage aren't conducted against the DPRK in the future. These statements must be formal and official. If the U.S. continues to deny this and doesn't issue these statements, we will be dead with severity.

I ask for you to help in any way possible that we may live together again in happiness and peace. Don't lose your faith as I know God is with us. If I am able to return home, I want to become a minister. I don't want to hurt anyone, but want to help people.

He concluded his letter by quoting "More things are wrought by prayer than this world dreams of."

Since so many people had expressed concern about Frank, Janice decided to share the letter with the *Pottsville Republican*. She was forced to form a difficult opinion when a reporter asked her to comment on the letter.

"I don't believe we can apologize to a Communist nation as simply as the letter implies," she told him thoughtfully. "I think that if the United States did apologize, it would put the crewmen's lives in jeopardy. And if we apologize when there is no need, it would make us liars."

The reporter asked her what else she thought could be done. Janice hesitated only a few seconds. "I plead with everyone to pray for the release of the crewmen," she said. "I have no confidence in man's ability to settle such matters, as the world situation shows that man is unable to bring peace. I believe only in the power of God and earnest prayer to solve the situation."

Why did her husband write such words, the reporter wanted to know.

"I know he would never write a letter of that nature unless under duress," was her firm reply.

As for Steve Harris's wife, the strange letters only stirred up the anxiety that had possessed her since the capture became known. She knew there was a great deal of secrecy and responsibility involved with Steve's duties aboard the *Pueblo,* though he had never been able to talk even to her about it. She could not keep her mind from speculating on what special treatment the Koreans might reserve for him. How much information did he possess—and how desperate would they be to get it? The troubled look on his face in the vision she had had haunted her. To avoid the probing questions of reporters and the possibility that she might say something which would jeopardize Steve or the crew, Esther moved from the nation's capital to a small community in the state of Washington, in an apartment near another brother. This way she would be on the coast when the *Pueblo* crewmen were released, a hope she voiced in every prayer.

Steve's mother, until she learned his duties from newspaper reports, was not aware of the intelligence role he played aboard the *Pueblo*. But she had no intention of standing by while her son was appealing for help. In April she penned a letter to each of the hundred U. S. Senators:

> As the distraught mother of a fine young officer captured aboard the U.S.S. *Pueblo*, I have waited in vain for nearly twelve weeks for some word of progress by our government. *Pueblo's* eighty-two men are threatened with "execution" as stated in letters home to parents and wives, "unless our President apologizes and meets certain conditions." What is keeping him? What have *you* done to save these men?
>
> While our Navy advisers at local levels right on up to Secretary of the Navy Paul R. Ignatius have tried to comfort us anxious parents, we want progress, not comfort. "Doing everything possible" seems to boil down to only one avenue of hope; i.e., negotiations at Panmunjom (which must be "carried on in secret" to be effective). While we parents appreciate the need for secrecy, after thirteen such meetings, where are we?
>
> What is our sons' captors' price for eighty-two lives? What ransom has been offered? There is only one thing they are asking —an apology. These eighty-two highly-trained young Navy men love their country well. During these long, anxious weeks of incarceration, how many times have they asked the agonizing questions: Has my country forgotten me? Are they about to let me die through sheer negligence of my live-or-die request?
>
> Last night on the newscast by Huntley-Brinkley, documents were shown of the *Pueblo's* records purportedly proving the ship *was* in North Korean territorial waters. Whether or not this eventually proves to be the truth, *this entire nation would understand why our President is apologizing*—if he so chooses.

I continue to have implicit faith in the power of my great country to resolve this dilemma with honor and dignity. In the case of the *Pueblo*, however, we are dealing with an "outlaw regime" (quotation from Rear Admiral Smith). Even outlaws can lose their patience.

An apology is about as "peaceful" a solution as one could find. Please get busy before it's too late!

Sincerely and gratefully,
Eleanor Van Buskirk Harris

In July she suggested in another letter to every Senator: "Isn't it possible to use the 'language of diplomacy' in forging an 'apology' which would guarantee the safe return of our men—alive?" She pointed out that "our country saved the lives of two men, Captain Carleton Voltz and Captain Ben Stutts, by offering false apologies. Is it any more 'dishonorable' to save the lives of eighty-two hand-picked, highly-trained valorous men?" She had started the letter with a prescient plea: "Consider the all-important face-saving request of *Pueblo's* captors—an apology. You'll have to come to it, sooner or later."

She sent letters to the executive branch of the government as well as the legislative, and got friends and relatives to join her desperate campaign. In reply, Mrs. Harris received personal letters from Rear Admiral John V. Smith, truce negotiator at Panmunjom; Secretary of State Dean Rusk; Massachusetts Senator Edward Kennedy; and other Senators (including Robert F. Kennedy just a week before his assassination). She was granted a personal meeting with the Secretary of State and came away from the visit encouraged that the government would be glad to apologize if it felt that doing so would effect the release of the men. But she now realized the multitude of other conditions involved.

The insurmountability of the problem stunned her. Yet it precipitated the return to a faith in God that she felt she had grown away from. Clearly, the final outcome was in God's hands. A room in her home became a special prayer room. She wrote Admiral

Mrs. Lloyd Bucher, wife of the Pueblo captain, prepared Christmas celebration in hopes her husband would be released for the holiday.
UPI

Smith that eighty-two mothers and wives would be going to the conference table with him, praying that God would put the right words in his mouth. She sent inspirational quotes and Bible passages to her son. One that seemed to her to sharply define Steve's crucial test of faith was Hebrews 12:5-7:

> My son, despise not thou the chastening of the Lord, nor faint when thou art rebuked of him: for whom the Lord loveth he chasteneth, and scourgeth every son whom he receiveth. If ye endure chastening, God dealeth with you as with sons; for what son is he whom the father chasteneth not?

Other concerned citizens, including Rose Bucher, the *Pueblo* captain's wife, were determined not to let the government forget the American crewmen. Committees were formed to keep America mindful of the imprisoned *Pueblo* crew. "Remember the Pueblo" signs appeared. Churches held prayer gatherings for the crew's release. In San Diego fourteen-year-old Marcee Rethwish organized two gigantic *Pueblo* prayer meetings—on the hundredth and two hundredth days of the captivity—each attracting 1,500 people to Balboa Park.

The *Pueblo* wives and mothers watched and waited and prayed. But as the days plodded on, doubts sometimes assailed them. On July 23 Janice Ginther telegrammed the President:

> Today is my birthday and what a wonderful gift—for it is six months today since the *Pueblo* was seized. My husband is a crew member and I think it is about time this country does something to bring about their release. How do I know my husband is still alive? If there is progress, why does the State Department deny it? What do I tell my little girl when she cries for her father? What kind of future do we have? Aren't those eighty-two lives important? What about all the families that are involved? I'm tired of hearing "be patient." You can't possibly realize what a terrible nightmare this is. Please get those crewmen back soon.

Janice was to learn that the best antidote for her despondency was not provocative prose but patient prayer. As she renewed her trust in God, her confidence that the crewmen would be returned

Members of the National Committee for Responsible Patriotism and other groups march in New York's Columbus Circle to dramatize demands for the release of the crew of the Pueblo.

UPI Telephoto

became complete. To speed the days of waiting, she turned to the Bible and religious books and magazines, often quoting from them when she wrote to Frank. In August she acted on her belief that her husband would be released. She moved with her daughter into an apartment, a simple forty-dollar-a-month row house across the street from his folks, to await his return.

When October painted its annual extravagance of color on the wooded Appalachian hills surrounding Pottsville, Janice appreciated God's handiwork. The human design had been annoyingly imperfect. The coal furnace, banked for heat through the chilly nights, insistently overheated the house during the Indian summer days. Then the car started acting up. Janice had taken it to a garage only to learn it would take a day to repair.

She was waiting for transportation home when Lou Grossman, a high school friend of Frank's, introduced himself. Since her picture had appeared in the *Republican,* Janice had gotten used to being recognized by Pottsville citizens. She thought little about the encounter.

Later in the day, however, Grossman called to say he had seen a picture of some *Pueblo* crewmen in a magazine. Frank's father, along with Frank's mother and sister, drove Janice and Bonnie to the garage. They entered the outer office, where Grossman greeted them with a copy of the October 18 issue of *Time.* He held it open at page 38.

The group studied the picture carefully. Frank wasn't in it, but at least it represented a contact with him. Janice read the caption.

> The North Koreans are having a hard time proving to the world that the captive crewmen of the U.S.S. *Pueblo* are a contrite and cooperative lot. Last week Pyongyang's flocks tried again—and lost to the U.S. Navy. In this class-reunion picture, three of the crewmen have managed to use the medium for a message, furtively getting off the U. S. hand signal of obscene derisiveness and contempt.

"Oh, no!" she moaned. "If the Koreans read this, those crewmen are going to be in trouble."

5

DECEMBER 23

The crew couldn't explain it. After eight months of Orwellian terror, the beatings had suddenly stopped. The food, though unimproved in quality, was served in greater quantity. Cookies, candy, and beer were added to the menu. The Americans were taken to theatrical events in the capital city. Rigid rules were relaxed.

The Korean explanation had been that the *Pueblo* crew had "repented." They were sorry for the wrong they had done, and now they could expect good treatment. But Navy scuttlebutt, still very active in confinement, held the view that the Koreans had satisfied their progaganda desires, a concession of some sort had been made, and the crew would soon be released.

As October stretched into November, however, the Americans became apprehensive. They felt like shipwrecked tourists stranded in a remote country, grudgingly tolerated by uneasy hosts while awaiting their uncertain transport. The men became restive. No longer required to stick together in common suffering, they discovered faults in one another. Petty grievances were magnified. The hostility that months of poor food and torture had fostered came to the surface. Quarrels became frequent. In some cases blows, once dealt by the captors, were now exchanged with each other.

December came, and with it a change in the Korean temperament. Near midmonth the entire crew was called into the theater. It looked as if another speech from the "Glorious General" awaited them. He had lectured to them before through an interpreter for periods as long as half a day. He could never say enough about the glories of Communist living. The determined look on his face this time, however, was not the genial air he had exhibited in recent doctrinaire sermons.

He got right to the point. It seemed that one of the photos released to the American press had hand signals "of obscene derisiveness and contempt." Western news organs were also speculating on the meaning of the "strange confessions" filled as they were with sly phrases and improbable admissions. This called for appropriate treatment for the *Pueblo* crew, of course. There would have to be new interrogations, revised confessions.

Memories of the Barn were rekindled, only this time it was worse. The crew's room consignments were increased from eight to twelve men, and the Koreans used the vacated areas for interrogation rooms. In their crowded quarters the Americans were required to sit through the day in their chairs, heads lowered in an attitude of submission, speaking to one another prohibited. Before they could move—to visit the bathroom or even to blow the nose —they had to respectfully ask permission. The complement of Korean guards was augmented to better check on the crew's compliance to the new regulations. The guards roamed the barracks, inspecting with maliciously probing eyes their captives' deportment and making the passage to the bathroom a gauntlet of sadistic horror.

As the Americans sat for hours—their throats constricted from the unusual head angle, their stretched neck muscles demanding a shift of cranial position, their buttocks protesting the hardness of the chair seats, their bladders unrelieved for fear of the bathroom trip—they could hear from the interrogation rooms and the hallways the thuds and whaps of Korean boot blows and whippings, the screams and moans of their pleading comrades. Brief respites for unpalatable meals were welcomed, as was the evening's wearied rest. But at six every morning it would start all over again.

As they entered the prisoners' rooms the guards, no longer
the tolerant benefactors they had been over the past two months,
seemed eager to punish the slightest misdemeanor. Ginther got it
for no reason he could pinpoint. He had been sitting with down-
cast head, his eyes staring sightlessly at his folded hands, his
Timex returning the blank gaze, its hands forever indicating noon-
time . . . or midnight. Perhaps he flinched when the guard strode
by; maybe his head was not quite in the right position. But something wasn't acceptable. The first kick against his temple spurred
a strong impulse to retaliate, but Ginther subdued it. He knew
that eighty-two lives, not just his own, were in jeopardy. He re-
tucked his chin, but the second kick was on its way. The heavy
boot tore into his already-bruised flesh. He bit his lips and closed
his smarting eyes tightly, praying that he wouldn't do anything
foolish. Satisfied at last, the guard walked on.

The vengeance of the Koreans reached its climax in the interrogations aimed at gaining new confessions. As he was led down
the hallway, Lieutenant Harris prayed that God would see him
through the ordeal and that he would be enabled to answer the
questions in a way that would bring no damage to the United
States. In the Barn, he well remembered, painful punishment had
effectively been inflicted without leaving visible wounds. The
guards had carefully avoided hitting the heads of those who were
to be seen in propaganda photographs and televised confessions.
But Harris soon learned that this time no area of the body was
to be left unpummeled.

The choicest torment was reserved for those who had been
photographed in what was to become known as the "hand picture." Quartermaster First-Class Chuck Law was one. He was
made to take a kneeling position in front of the interrogator's
table and was then struck repeatedly across the shoulders and
back with a two-by-two-inch board four feet long. On one of the
blows the club broke in two. The two pieces were then used until
they also broke. A four-by-four was brought in and used until

Law slumped to the floor, to be kicked, punched, and cuffed by the guards. Another gesturing sailor received the chair-above-the-head kneeling punishment that Ginther had experienced—but with a thick stick cutting into the tendons behind his knees.

As were most of the *Pueblo* crewmen, Harris was praying intensely. He asked God to frustrate the Koreans' attempts to harm the Americans and to see them through the renewed torture. He was afraid that some who had only recently put their trust in God would now turn from him in misplaced blame for their sufferings. A weird, impractical, improbable thought entered his mind and he expressed it silently in prayer. "Let us get home by Christmas."

On the eighth morning of the general's protracted revenge for the hand picture and the doctored confessions the guards failed to come en masse as usual, and those who did show up were smiling. The torture had ceased as abruptly as it had begun. Not only did the interrogations and the beatings stop, but the food ration was again increased and the *Pueblo* corpsmen, along with Korean doctors and nurses, were set to caring for the newly wounded. The Koreans again explained their changed attitude by saying the Americans were now "sincerely repentant" and could be forgiven. The medical work, so feverishly set upon, however, appeared to be a desperate patch-up attempt. Attention was concentrated on wounds that showed and injuries that caused noticeable impairment. Hot paraffin, used to reduce swelling, was applied only to the visible bruises. Either the barracks was due for a UN inspection, the crew reasoned, or they were really going to be released this time. Such a possibility was dangerous even to think about, they knew, because false hope was more damaging in its frustration than no hope at all.

The Koreans devilishly tantalized their captives with the prospect of freedom. "Your government has agreed to make an apology," they would tell them. Then they would claim that the U.S. was stalling on the agreement. To obscure the picture, they would add, "We don't know whether the apology will come during the Johnson administration or if it will come under the Nixon administration." The crew wanted desperately to believe that a release would be effected soon, but they had been wrong on that assumption before. Yet the hurried patch-up work, if the Koreans were indeed serious about a U.S. apology, surely indicated that release might be soon. At least it seemed more certain than ever before. By Korean design, the Americans were thoroughly confused. If they could only know what to believe . . . or dare to hope.

The anticipation of returning home nonetheless provided a release from the memories of the harrowing days just past, a period referred to, quite naturally, as "Hell Week." When they could bring themselves to talk about it, the crewmen repeated a common experience during the torment, that of constant prayer. Even those who up to that point had not expressed themselves in such intercourse talked about their petitions to God. Ginther was pleased that some he had pointed toward Christ were now proclaiming the Savior's presence and help in their time of deep need.

Chief Kell had perhaps the most unusual experience to share. In October he had started what he called a "special novena" that God would let them be home with their families by Christmas. His prayer every night was, "Dear God, if it be your will, let us make it home for Christmas. And let me honor your Son's birth in the proper way. Not here in this prison, but in a house of God."

During Hell Week, although he had almost decided it was not God's will that they make it home for the holiday, he continued to pray for a release. He recalled one prayer in particular: "Dear God, I'm not losing any faith in you, but please give us some sign that we can know you'll get us home. Christmas is only a week away now, and—if you're going to get us out—please do it soon, for we've got to get home!"

His most fervent prayer was made the night before Hell Week ended; he took the cessation of the beatings as his sign. "We're going to make it home! I know it!" he told the others. The thing

Rear Admiral John Smith (center, left) senior delegate of the United Nations Command to the Armistice Commission in January, 1968, delivers formal protest against the seizure of the Pueblo to North Korean delegates at Panmunjom.

Major General Gilbert H. Woodward, senior United Nations Command delegate on December 23, 1968, addressing newsmen at the time of the signing of the document which effected release of Pueblo crew.

UPI Radiophoto

that capped his certainty was his knowledge that that one crewman who had gone through the whole confinement period without offering a prayer to God had at last started praying.

The optimism of the ever-smiling Kell was not shared by every one in the crew. His confidence, after all, hadn't yet opened the prison gate.

Even as the *Pueblo* crewmen were discussing their future, another verbal exchange a hundred miles south of them had been dealing with the same subject. At Panmunjom in the United Nations Command territory, American and North Korean negotiators were near accord on one of the most unusual agreements in history. The discussions were to culminate in a few days with Major General Gilbert H. Woodward, chief U.S. negotiator, reading a strange statement before Korean and American witnesses and newsmen:

"The *Pueblo* was not engaged in illegal activity . . . . We could not apologize for actions which we did not believe took place . . . . The document which I am going to sign was prepared by the North Koreans and is at variance with the above position, but my signature will not and cannot alter the facts. I will sign the document to free the crew and only to free the crew."

General Woodward then signed the paper. It read in part:

> The Government of the United States of America, acknowledging the validity of the confessions of the crew of the U.S.S. *Pueblo* . . . shoulders full responsibility and solemnly apologizes for the grave acts of espionage committed by the U.S. ship against the Democratic People's Republic of Korea . . . .

The agreed-to "validity of the confessions" was a left-handed victory for the North Koreans. In the *Pueblo's* log, which they had doctored and upon which the crewmen had confessed trespass, were two entries which indicated that the ship had covered 500 nautical miles in twelve minutes. This would have required a speed of 2,500 knots. North Korean charts gave coordinates for the *Pueblo's* position just before capture which would have put the ship variously thirty-two miles inland in North Korea and six miles aground on the Japanese island of Kyushu—400 miles from where the *Pueblo* was captured.

The agreement concluded:

> . . . Simultaneously with the signing of this document the undersigned acknowledges receipt of eighty-two former crew members of the *Pueblo* and one corpse.

It was duly signed and dated—23 December 1968. A Monday, two days before Christmas.

Since Thursday, when Hell Week ended, the American captives had been spitefully kept in suspense about the possibility of repatriation. On Sunday morning, however, they had been called again to the theater where their last meeting, on the eleventh, had marked the start of Hell Week. An entirely different atmosphere was present this time. The officer who read the announcement could not conceal his own excitement in proclaiming, "Tomorrow you will be released." The room reverberated with the shouts of the Americans. Backs were pounded. Handshakes were exchanged. Joyful tears were shed. Hatred of the Koreans almost dissolved. The duty officer who was trying to deliver further instructions looked halfway human. But could they believe him this time? The doubts returned.

Before the Americans would leave the building there was to be a final news conference (this time the crewmen put on a splendid exhibition of contrition for their monstrous crimes and appreciation of their captors' willingness to forgive) and a final meeting with the Glorious General (in the exchange of lies the general admonished the Americans not to forget their humane treatment). That evening their doubts dissolved as the crewmen were stripped and searched, issued new uniforms with heavy coats and winter caps, and marched to waiting buses. This was it.

The bus ride to the railroad station was not marked with levity, except for a joyous air of expectancy, because the crew did not want to lose what they had waited so long to gain. On the train, its windows curtained as were those on the bus, the men were given individual berths for the all-night ride. Few could sleep, though, from anticipation of what the day would bring. The train arrived in Kaesong the next morning and the crew again boarded buses for the ten-mile drive to the bridge that spans the armistice line between North and South Korea.

The captain was called from the lead bus for a long ceremonious inspection of the rough-hewn casket holding Duane Hodges' body and the identification of the remains. While the crewmen waited in the cold buses, Commander Bucher stood for more than an hour on the colder, snow-covered ground in his canvas shoes. Finally, a North Korean general emerged from the building that stood at the North Korean end of the bridge. The officer screamed at Bucher for another twenty minutes. As cold as the men were in the buses, they knew that the captain's feet were freezing while he stood listening to yet another half hour of translation.

When Bucher returned to the bus he joined the final repetition of the hours-long recital of instructions that the crew had been receiving. The North Koreans wanted to insure there would be no last-minute loss of face. The Americans were told that an imaginary circle encompassing the bridge and the camps on either side outlined a joint security area and that either force could make arrests within it. Then they were given a list of things that were prohibited, including the display of provocative gestures, smoking, laughing, reading, writing, and eliminating. They were told to answer "yes, sir" loudly when their names were called and to march across the bridge without running or looking back. North Korean machine guns were ready to enforce the regulations.

The captain was the first to cross. He was followed in reverse seniority by the men and officers. The crewmen had been made so tense by the final North Korean instructions that after screaming "Yes, sir!" at the call of their names, they walked stiffly across the bridge in zombie-like tread, afraid that the progress might be stopped at any moment. Their faces registered both fear

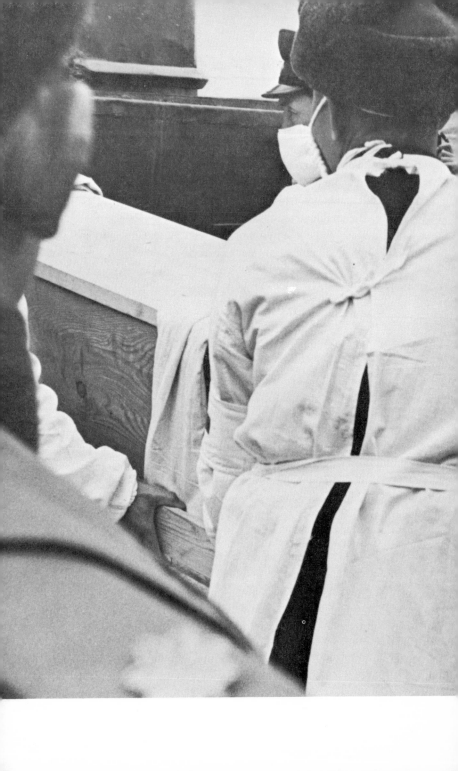

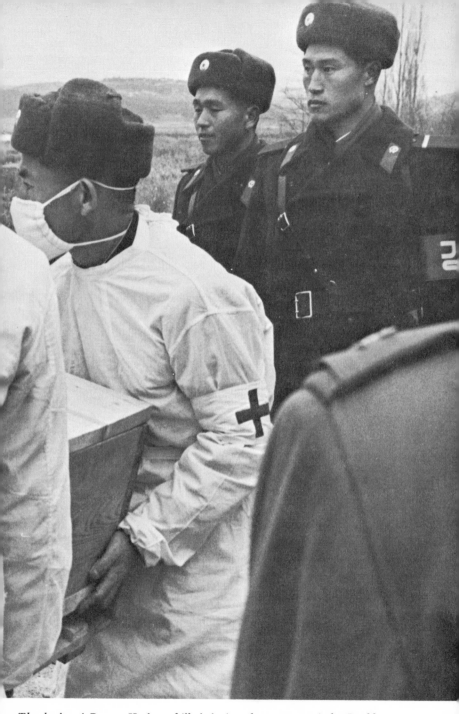

The body of Duane Hodges, killed during the capture of the Pueblo, was transferred in this wooden box during the release of the crew.
U.S. Navy

Pueblo crewmen file across the "Bridge of No Return" between North Korean (background) and South Korean territories in the demilitarized zone to awaiting American buses—and freedom.

U.S. Navy

*The first man across the bridge at Panmunjom upon the release of the
Pueblo crew was the captain, Commander Lloyd Bucher.*

and disbelief. To the waiting Americans the *Pueblo* crewmen appeared to be half-human creatures, undernourished and emotionally drained. To the repatriates the rescuers looked superhuman, well-fed, and marvelously able to smile in genuine friendship. When each man reached the South Korean side, Commander Bucher greeted him with a handshake and a pat on the back.

As the sixty-fourth man across the bridge entered the safety of the South, he heard the man in front of him ask, "Is it okay to yell? My emotions are ready to explode, but I sure don't want them to call us back!"

"Better keep 'em in check for a while," he was told. "We're still in the joint security area."

Then Ginther stepped up to be greeted. It seemed important for him to know the time of his repatriation. He quietly asked the healthy-looking American soldier the time of day. As he did so, he looked again at his own timepiece, useless without its energy cell. "It's straight up twelve," the soldier told him. Ginther muttered and shook his head disbelievingly at the bewildered G.I. The sailor didn't bother interpreting his actions. How could he explain that for months every time he glanced at his watch he had been looking at the hour of his deliverance?

The last American captive to cross the bridge to freedom was the Executive Officer, Lt. Edward R. Murphy. Ahead of him was the Intelligence Officer. Lt. Harris would always carry the image of that moment with him. The bleak countryside. The bridge spanning the sandy creek bed. The light snow cover underfoot. The cold breeze. His footsteps were measured. He didn't want anything to go wrong now. But could it? God had brought them this far; he would guide them safely the rest of the way. An overwhelming sense of gratitude engulfed him then as it must have every one making that slow journey. His soul was singing a doxology of praise. There was to come an opportunity that night to raise his voice in an expression of his thankfulness. He would be enabled then, too, to see the climax of a spiritual journey that

Able to smile again, Lieutenant Harris, still in Korean uniform, stands before American military bus at Panmunjom.

The tenseness of the walk across the freedom bridge is shown on the face of Frank Ginther shortly after repatriation.   U.S. Navy

had begun with the meager response to his attempt to lead a worship service aboard the *Pueblo*. At the united worship service held at the 121st Air Evacuation Hospital near Seoul that evening, every crew member participated wholeheartedly.

But now the crewmen were being gathered into groups. The Red Cross had welcoming kits for each one. The bags contained simple things—candy, gum, toothbrushes, shaving gear—but their significance was not lost. These things were *American*. The men were given Army overcoats and boarded onto buses. At last they were heading out of the joint security area. The crewmen could contain themselves no longer. Shouted invectives directed toward the North Koreans were drowned in the outbursts of pure joy. The men hugged each other, tossed their Korean caps, and continued to shout. Many stripped their outer garments in favor of the Army overcoats, trampling the North Korean issue underfoot. Everyone got the jumble of thoughts out of his emancipated brain at the top of his lungs. It was virtually impossible to know what another was saying, but it didn't matter. Above the turmoil Ginther thought he heard his name. He strained against the conglomeration of sounds.

"Frank!" the voice was saying, "you were right. God brought us through!" It was Abelon, he thought. There was too much turmoil to know for sure, but he had gotten the message. It had come upon the others, too. Here and there heads were being lowered. This was no mere diplomatic coup by their native land that they were experiencing, no merciful release by condescending captors. Their repatriation was a gracious act by a sovereign God. It had come when the captives had at last recognized that their only hope was in him. None was bitter at God. They well realized the horrifying results possible when God is shut out of a people's lives. Their thankfulness was genuine and complete. Ginther felt a special gratitude that God had guided him back into his paths of righteousness and had enabled him to point others to the Way,

As North Korean guards watch closely, Pueblo crewman Norman
Spear crosses the bridge to freedom.

U.S. Navy

Pueblo crewmen board helicopter for trip from Panmunjom to Seoul. In the line to board are, left to right, Communications Technicians Anthony Lamantia, Earl Kisler, and Harry Lewis.

the Truth, and the Life.

Then as the shouts diminished Ginther heard again, "Frank!"

"Yeah?"

"Frank—say a prayer."

The first American meal in eleven months for the Pueblo crew was to have been steak—but doctors decided noodle soup would be better because of the repatriates' weakened condition. No one complained. Pictured are Communications Technician Charles Ayling (left) and Communications Chief James Kell.

Marching into the crowd of anxious wives, parents and relatives in San Diego, Pueblo crewmen are welcomed to their homeland on Christmas eve.

UPI

Pueblo Electrician Lawrence Strickland gets a welcome he'll long re-member upon his arrival in America.

Lieutenant Harris walks with his mother, Mrs. Eleanor Harris, shortly after the crew's arrival home.

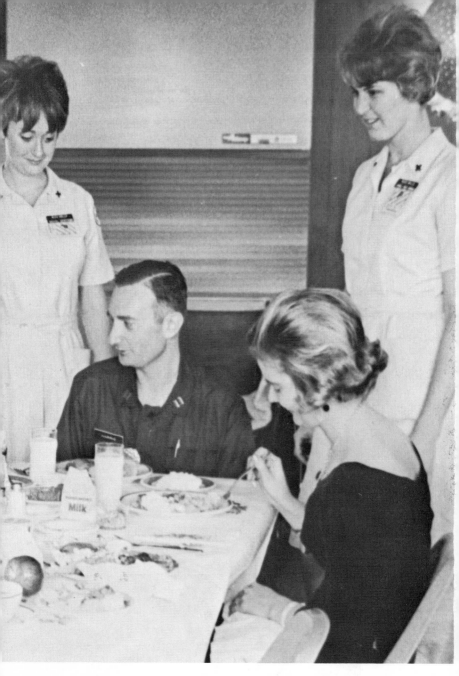

Enjoying Christmas dinner served to the crew of the Pueblo and their families are (left to right) Mrs. Mary A. McClintock; Communications Technician Ralph McClintock; Mrs. Eleanor Harris, mother of Lieutenant Harris; Harris; and his wife Esther. Standing by are Red Cross social workers.

U.S. Navy

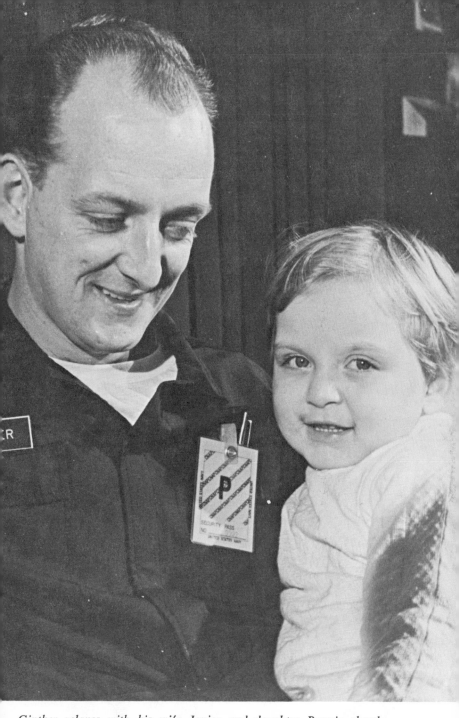

Ginther relaxes with his wife Janice and daughter Bonnie shortly after their reunion in San Diego.

*Back home in Pottsville, Pennsylvania, Frank Ginther rejoins his
mother, father, and sister Margaret (left).*

Pottsville Republican

*In Melrose, Massachusetts, Steve Harris—shown with his wife Esther
—is feted at welcome home party in his mother's home.*

Photo by the author

EPILOGUE

Military jet transports out of Seoul, Korea, soared westward over the Pacific with their eighty-two priority passengers. The airborne crossing seemed much smoother than the surface voyage the same men had taken a year earlier. They were heading home now—home for Christmas. The duplicity and intrigue that had frustrated the crewmen of the U.S.S. *Pueblo* for eleven months had ended.

A month later—during a Navy court of inquiry convened in Coronado, California, in late January, 1969—their experiences were excruciatingly but dutifully relived. When Commander Lloyd Bucher recited the horror of their imprisonment, he answered questions about his forced confession that the crewmen themselves had wondered about.

Following repeated beatings, Bucher told the court, he had been taken into an interrogation room and presented with a confession. Through an interpreter, he was told by Colonel "Super-C," who later became the "Glorious General," that if he signed the document, he and his men would be returned home quickly. Bucher refused. He described the scene:

"I was given two minutes to sign or be shot. Then they made me kneel on the floor. I knelt down, facing the wall, and an officer with a pistol drew back the slide and stood behind me. . . . Super-C said, 'You have two minutes to sign the confession or be shot.' I was somewhat relieved at the prospect of being shot without being tortured. At this point I thought it would be a blessing. I knew it is possible through human torture to get somebody to say anything, whether he means it or not."

Bucher paused. "I knelt there on the floor," he started—and then his voice broke.

"Would you like a recess at this time?" the court asked.

"No, sir. I would rather get this over with right now, if I might. I'm sure I can do it." There was a long silence. Bucher took a drink of water, then continued:

"I spent two minutes on the floor and repeated over and over . . . the phrase. . . ." He paused again, took several deep breaths and sipped some more water. ". . . the phrase, 'I love you, Rose.' I thought this would keep my mind off what was going to happen. At the end of two minutes they asked me again if I was ready to sign. I said I would not sign. Then he [Super-C] told the officer at my side to move, apparently so that when I was shot, and the bullet passed through my head, it would not hit the officer standing in front me.

"Then the colonel said: 'Kill the s.o.b.!' So the gun was clicked. Then the interpreter said, 'Well, it was a misfire. You will have another two minutes. You were lucky the last time.' I had fully expected to be shot, but when the slide was drawn back, presumably to insert another bullet, and I did not hear any bullet hit the floor, I knew it was a game they were playing with me, and they weren't going to kill me.

"The two minutes went by and I refused to confess. Then the colonel said I wasn't worth a bullet, and I would be beaten to death. They turned to and beat me and kicked me, and they worked me over real good. They beat me to the floor, and I lost consciousness after a few minutes. . . .

"Then I was carried out to my room and thrown on the bed. . . . I asked permission to go to the bathroom, and they marched me to the head. All I could urinate was blood."

A long pause followed. "At ten o'clock that night, Chipmunk [an interpreter] and Super-C came with drawn pistols and told me they would show me what happens to spies. . . . I was led up half a flight of stairs, and then down again into a semi-basement.

"A South Korean was there with a strap around his chest, strapped to the wall. They explained to me that he was a South

Korean spy. He was alive, but had been through a terrible ordeal. He had a compound fracture of the upper right arm. The bone was sticking out. He was stripped to the waist. He had completely bitten through. . . ." Bucher coughed and then went on. "He had completely bitten through his lower lip, and his lower lip was hanging down from the side of his mouth. His right eye had been put out. His head was hanging down. There was a lot of . . . black matter which had run out of his eye and down his right cheek. His face was badly swollen. . . . He was under three spotlights. . . .

"Then I was taken back to the interrogation room. . . . They asked me if I knew I was responsible for the lives of my crew, and I answered 'yes' . . . and told them they had murdered one of my men. . . . I received a blow that sent me across the room for that statement." At this point Bucher had sensed desperation in his interrogator. "I felt it was urgent for him to get some sort of confession in order to . . . justify the piracy they had committed. . . . He said, 'We will now begin to shoot your crew one at a time in your presence until you sign, and if you do not sign you know we have the means to persuade you.'

"I was not prepared to see my crew shot. They said they would start with the youngest man first and they would shoot them in order and they had already sent for Bland [Engineman Howard E. Bland, 21]. I was convinced they would do it. I was convinced they were animals. I was just not prepared for this type of mental torture. I was convinced they were desperate to get a confession and would shoot my men. I told them at this time I would sign this confession, and I did sign it. Then I was taken back to my room and brought a huge tray of food, eggs, and other goodies. I did not touch it."

Anxious weeks of waiting and wondering followed the conclusion of the inquiry. The crewmen were admonished not to release information to reporters until the deliberations of the court had been completed. In May, with Secretary of the Navy John H. Chaffee's exoneration of the *Pueblo* captain and crew, many of the crewmen were once again asked to relive their bizarre imprisonment, this time to satisfy an American press hungry for more information.

Strangely, the men were willing — almost eager — to comply. Much about their imprisonment had yet to be explained. The court of inquiry, they felt, had raised disturbing questions about the conduct of the *Pueblo's* senior officers. The crew wanted to clear these misunderstandings and to expound on their experiences which had not been a concern of the court. What the Americans had learned about life in a Communist state was not relevant to the inquiry. The overwhelming spiritual dimension of the Korean confinement was not a proper matter to be examined by the court. But such revelations were of supreme importance to many crewmen. In their answers to interviewers or in their own published accounts of the capture and captivity, a declaration, uttered independently and in various words, was repeated with startling frequency. "I never lost faith in my captain, my country, or my God."

In every experience of life—be it beautiful or boring, fruitful or frustrating, pleasant or painful—there are lessons to be learned. It was to discover the lesson of the *Pueblo* that one reporter who had studied the published testimony of the Navy inquiry began to interview the crewmen. On one occasion he sat in a quiet motel room in a Boston suburb, talking with Lt. Steve Harris, the *Pueblo's* intelligence officer.

Harris, as well as the other crewmen interviewed, exhibited no bitterness over the incident. He professed his desire to continue to serve his country as a military officer and emphasized his loyalty and devotion to his captain, Commander Bucher. Gifted with remarkable recall ability, the lieutenant explained as much about his experiences on the ship and during captivity as naval security and his own sensitivities would permit. In giving his assessment of the ordeal, Harris revealed—as did the others interviewed— much about the character of the *Pueblo* crewmen:

"We were fully prepared and would have been quite willing to die for our country. . . . We suffered instead. But we came through with a greater sense of values, I believe. Before the ordeal I was just one of many naval officers. I knew the country needed military men for its system of defense. *Now* I know what we are defending ourselves against.

"We were eyewitnesses to the horrors of Communism, what it really does to people, and how evil a system it really is. Now we can appreciate our country—with all its faults—and what it stands for. I wouldn't wish the experience on anyone, but if the people here could go through what we went through, they'd know what they have in a free country."

In his simple, brief delivery of sentiments echoed by fellow crewmen, the Intelligence Officer of the U.S.S. *Pueblo* had eloquently expressed why this book had to be written.

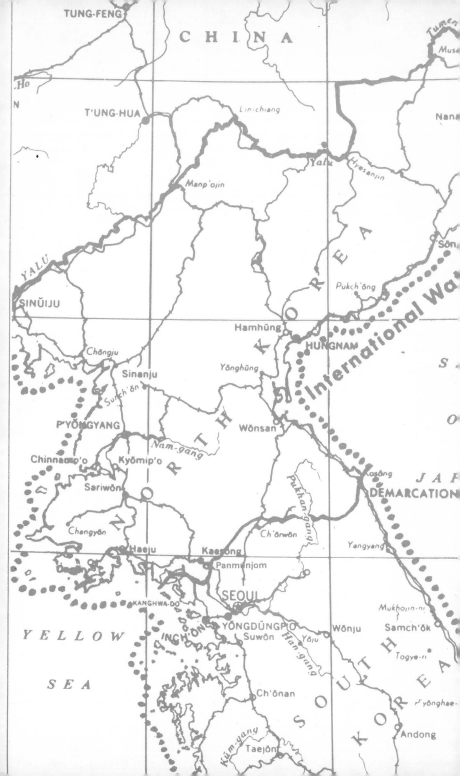